Proclaiming the Great Ends
of the Church

Also by Joseph D. Small
From Geneva Press

Conversations with the Confessions:
Dialogue in the Reformed Tradition (editor)

Fire and Wind: The Holy Spirit in the Church Today (editor)

Proclaiming the Great Ends of the Church

of the Church

Mission and Ministry for Presbyterians

JOSEPH D. SMALL, EDITOR

Geneva Press
Louisville, Kentucky

First edition
Published by Geneva Press
Louisville, Kentucky

10 11 12 13 14 15 16 17 18 19—10 9 8 7 6 5 4 3 2 1

Book design by Sharon Adams
Cover design by Eric Walljasper, Minneapolis, MN

Library of Congress Cataloging-in-Publication Data

Proclaiming the great ends of the church : mission and ministry for Presbyterians / Joseph D. Small, editor. — 1st ed.
   p. cm.
  ISBN 978-0-664-50307-9 (alk. paper)
  1. Presbyterian Church (U.S.A.)—Doctrines.   2. Preaching.   3. Missions.   4. Mission of the church.   I. Small, Joseph D.
  BX8969.5.P76   2010
  252'.05137—dc22

2009040105

Contents

Introduction

Joseph D. Small

*F*aithful proclamation of the gospel has always been at the center of Presbyterian life, and preaching remains a fundamental responsibility of the church's ministers. Preaching is not simply one item in a catalog of ministerial functions or a secondary activity in the bustle of congregational programs. Proclamation of the good news is at the heart of congregational life, a clear indicator of ecclesial fidelity. John Calvin, principal forebear of the Presbyterian Church's Reformed tradition, centers the church's faithful life in the gospel's proclamation through preaching and sacraments: "Wherever we see the Word of God purely preached and heard, and the sacraments administered according to Christ's institution, there, it is not to be doubted, a church of God exists."[1]

Calvin's formulation was not an abstract definition of an ideal, invisible church. He had actual, quite visible congregations in view. More specifically, his eyes were fixed on worshiping assemblies gathering week after week. So Calvin's question—and ours—is empirical: "When we look at a worshiping congregation, do we see and hear preaching that is faithful to the gospel? Do we see and hear and taste and feel celebrations of Baptism and the Lord's Supper that proclaim the good news?"

Focus on the real life of actual congregations is sharpened by Calvin's insertion of the two little words *and heard* into his formulation. He understood that proclamation of the Word alone is not sufficient, no matter how faithfully and skillfully preachers preach and teachers teach. Proclamation must be *heard* to fulfill its purpose. By hearing, Calvin did not mean mere listening, of course, or even mere understanding. *Hearing* means *receiving*, and *receiving* means *living out* the good news that is proclaimed in the preaching and teaching of the Word and in the celebration of Baptism and the Lord's Supper.

Proclamation of the Word of God centers the church on the grace of the Lord Jesus Christ, the love of God, and the communion of the Holy Spirit, and then calls the church to its reason for being, shaping its mission in the world. It is too often tempting and far too easy for ministers and congregations to turn inward, focusing on institutional success by developing programs to meet every real or imagined need and managing for growth. The preaching of God's Word pulls us away from self-absorption and organizational operations, drawing preachers and congregations into the good news of God's new Way in the world. David Buttrick puts the matter nicely: "Christian preaching tells a story and names a name. If narrative consciousness confers identity, then preaching transforms identity, converts in the truest sense of the word, by rewriting our stories into a God-with-us story—beginning, Presence, and end."[2]

But, in our time, the preaching of sermons is not always evaluated positively. Some thoughtful observers question whether sermons continue to be effective means of proclaiming the gospel, still capable of rewriting personal and congregational stories into a God-with-us story. We live in an age of quick, interactive communication—blogs, Facebook, and Twitter. Is a twenty-minute homily spoken to a voiceless gathering able to draw us into communion with the triune God, to set before us a world that is different from the way things are, and to project a way of life that is more real than the everyday existence that we assume to be factual?

The problematic of preaching goes far deeper than worries about various forms of current communication technology, however. Twenty-five years ago, Neil Postman examined the significance of "television culture" for the way we think. Postman maintains that all forms of communication media work in unobtrusive yet powerful ways to enforce their special definitions of reality: "Whether we are experiencing the world through the lens of speech or the printed word or the television camera, our media-metaphors classify the world for us, sequence it, frame it, enlarge it, reduce it, color it, argue a case for what the world is like."[3] Postman claims that television (and its ancillary expansions) has produced *The Age of Show Business*, in which entertainment is the primary lens through which we see the world. "The problem is not that television presents us with entertaining subject matter," says Postman, "but that all subject matter is presented as entertaining, which is another issue altogether."[4] Do we doubt it? A moment's reflection on the state of television news or the pervasive presence of reality(!) television is enough to confirm Postman's analysis.

What are the implications for preaching? Postman worries about what happens to preaching when it is presented on television, but the larger worry is what happens to preaching in churches where both preacher and congregation are shaped by a "television culture." Will the preacher be tempted, knowingly or unknowingly, to make the sermon "entertaining," providing people with something they want or think they want? Postman says what we should know without being told: "I believe I am not mistaken in saying that Christianity is a demanding and serious religion. When it is delivered as easy and amusing, it is another kind of religion altogether."[5] Even when the sermon is faithful to the truth of the gospel, will people in the congregation be bored by sustained thought or put off by demanding and serious preaching of the gospel?

The narrator of E. L. Doctorow's novel *The Waterworks*, looking back at the New York City of the 1870s, notes, "Quaint as it may seem, sermons in those days were considered newsworthy. The Monday papers were filled with them . . . substantial excerpts or even whole texts of representative sermons delivered from pulpits around town. The clergy were considered dignitaries of the city, and religious diction was assumed to be applicable to the public issues of the day."[6] Today, when even newspapers are becoming quaint, sermons are hardly newsworthy, and religious speech is consigned to the fringes of public issues.

Canadian theologian Douglas John Hall captures both the problematic of preaching and the daunting task of preachers:

> For in an age when human expectations with respect to public address have been reduced to entertainment, when slow argumentation and the reasoned presentation of ideas has been replaced by the shallow magic of the one-liner or the three minute "clip," and when individuals, if they are allowed to speak, speak as human beings whose natural endowments are "enhanced" by the techniques of sound, light, makeup, and all the rest, the person who dares to stand before others simply as a human being before human beings, attempting to sway them by mere language, knows the meaning of naked finitude.[7]

An entertainment/celebrity culture, coupled with a society that is both increasingly secular and religiously plural, raises difficult questions for Christian proclamation. Yet Reformed Christians have always made extravagant claims for preaching. The sixteenth-century Second Helvetic Confession boldly asserts, "THE PREACHING OF THE WORD OF GOD IS THE WORD OF GOD."[8] Twentieth-century theologian Karl Barth declares, "The Word of God preached now means . . . man's language about God, in which and through which God Himself speaks about Himself."[9] More recently, Andrew Purves contends that ". . . the reality, truth, and power of the actuality of our preaching is the Word of God, not an illustration of it, or some kind of practical application."[10]

These theological claims appear audacious, for most Presbyterians have heard enough dreadful sermons to doubt that God's voice resounds in preachers' mouths. Grand claims for preaching seem diminished when confronted by the reality of some careless, uninformed, opinionated, compliant, or self-serving sermons. Yet the claims for preaching do not depend on the wisdom or skill of those who speak but on their fidelity to the scriptural witness. What is implicit in all Reformed claims about preaching is made explicit in the Confession of 1967: "God instructs the church and equips it for mission through preaching and teaching. By these, when they are carried on in fidelity to the Scriptures and dependence upon the Holy Spirit, the people hear the word of God. . . ."[11] Note the clause *"when they are carried on in fidelity to the Scriptures and dependence upon the Holy Spirit."* The Directory for Worship is even more straightforward: "The preached Word or sermon is to be based upon the written Word. It is a proclamation of Scripture in the conviction that through the Holy Spirit Jesus Christ is present to the gathered people, offering grace and calling for obedience."[12]

Fidelity to Scripture is preacherly and congregational confidence that God has made himself known through Israel and in Jesus Christ, and that God's self-revelation finds authentic and reliable witness in the Old and New Testaments. Fidelity to Scripture is preacherly and congregational assurance that God continues to make himself known through the biblical word, and that the Holy Spirit is active in both the speaking of the preacher and the hearing of the congregation. To say that the preaching of the Word of God is the Word of God is not a grandiose claim for preaching but a confident declaration about the continuing presence of God.

Nearly ninety years ago Karl Barth pointed to the enduring significance of proclamation in the church. Having recently concluded his twelve-year pastorate in a small Swiss town, his address on the need of Christian preaching at a summer pastors' conference bore the marks of authentic experience.

> The serious meaning of the situation in our churches is that the people want to hear the word, that is, the answer to the question which, whether they know it or not, they are actually animated, Is it true? They want to find out and thoroughly understand the answer to this one question, Is it true? —and not some other answer which beats about the bush. . . . If we do not understand this ultimate desire, if we do *not* take the people seriously . . . we need not wonder if a majority of them, without becoming enemies of the church, gradually learn to leave the church to itself.[13]

Contemporary preaching, at its best, is animated by the same question: *Is it true?* In every sermon in every congregation, the truth of the gospel is at stake.

Proclaiming the Great Ends of the Church is a collection of sermons that represent a cross section of contemporary Presbyterian preaching. Most, though not all, were preached by pastors in the churches they serve. Some of the congregations that heard these sermons are large; some are small. Some of the preachers have been at it for many years, while others are in the very early years of ministry. The mix of preachers and congregations is multicultural and represents a broad spectrum of theological convictions. The collection is not only an attempt to be inclusive, however, but is also a means of showing how Presbyterian preachers fulfill their calling Sunday by Sunday in fidelity to Scripture and dependence on the Holy Spirit.

Although the sermons are rooted in specific scriptural texts, they address the themes found in the "Great Ends of the Church," a century-old statement of the foundational goals of church life. In our time, "vision statements" and "mission statements" have become a staple of church life. Congregations, presbyteries and synods, and national boards and agencies devise generalized statements of what they are to be and do. The process of developing mission statements may be valuable, but the results are almost always lackluster. Moreover, church mission statements are disturbingly similar to the mission statements of grocery stores and drug companies, featuring an idealized image, quality goods, and friendly service.

Perhaps Presbyterians would be better served by focusing attention on a "mission statement" that has been in the church's constitution for over one hundred years, such as the "Great Ends of the Church." Embedded in the opening chapter of the *Book of Order* are six great purposes of the church's life—the life of every congregation and of the whole denomination. Taken together, they express direction for mission with a clarity and substance rarely found in the fleeting products of church committees. The Great Ends of the Church are

> the proclamation of the gospel for the salvation of humankind; the shelter, nurture, and spiritual fellowship of the children of God; the maintenance of divine worship; the preservation of the truth; the promotion of social righteousness; the exhibition of the Kingdom of Heaven to the world.[14]

With an economy of words and a surplus of meaning, the church has six great aims to direct our life together, six basic works of the church that are foundational to who the church is and what the church is called to do.

The Great Ends of the Church should not be seen as a laundry list of disconnected items, for they are intended as a holistic vision for the church's life. The church cannot be faithful to the intention of the Great Ends by emphasizing some while neglecting others. All six of the church's great purposes are integrally related. Their interconnections become evident in an interesting way when they are paired from the outside in.

- "Proclamation of the gospel for the salvation of humankind" *and* "exhibition of the Kingdom of Heaven to the world." Senseless debates about verbal evangelism *vs.* the witness of our lives are put aside when their mutuality is made evident by the comprehensive design of the Great Ends. Speaking the gospel is oddly abstract without the witness of the Christian life; the witness of Christian life without the gospel narrative is vague and ambiguous. The Great Ends of the Church display their unity.
- "Shelter, nurture, and spiritual fellowship of the children of God" *and* "promotion of social righteousness." There need be no tension between the internal life and outward mission of the church. Focus on the inner life of a congregation or denomination without active engagement in the quest for social justice leads to self-seeking introversion, while focus on social action apart from attention to the inner life of the faith community leads to centrifugal exhaustion. The Great Ends of the Church display their unity.
- "Maintenance of divine worship" *and* "preservation of the truth." There should be no disjunction between devotion and integrity, drama and doctrine, beauty and truth. Worship that neglects the truth of the gospel, no matter how engaging and creative and inspiring it may be, is not maintaining the worship of *God*. Truth without praise and prayer is not truth about *God*. The Great Ends of the Church display their unity.

The Great Ends of the Church are not theological boilerplate, and fulfilling these six fundamental purposes is not automatic. Each of the Great Ends presents problems for the church and challenges for the preacher.

Proclamation of the gospel for the salvation of humankind: What exactly is the shape of the good news? The answer may seem self-evident to some individuals, but there is no shared articulation of "gospel" throughout the church or in most congregations. What is salvation? Is it forgiveness of sin? . . . eternal life in heaven? . . . abundant life in the here and now? . . . incorporation into the body of Christ? . . . all of the above? North American Christian consciousness of the religiously plural character of society leads to uncertainty about the universal truth of Christian faith. Is salvation only possible within the gospel of Jesus Christ? Little wonder that in a Lilly Endowment–sponsored survey of pastoral leaders, over 75 percent of respondents identified "difficulty of reaching people with the gospel today" as a problem in their ministry.[15]

Shelter, nurture, and spiritual fellowship of the children of God: Shelter from what? Nurture for growth into what? And in churches with fellowship halls and fellowship hours, what does *spiritual* fellowship mean? In a market-driven consumer culture, is there a danger that the inner life of the church will be shaped in ways designed to appeal to shoppers for religious goods and services? This seemingly benign Great End challenges the church to create a community that is radically different from common notions of togetherness. The church is called to be the one body of Christ, empowered by the one Spirit, living in one hope, with one Lord, one faith, one baptism, under one God and Father of all, who is above all and through all and in all (Eph. 4:4–6).

Maintenance of divine worship: The third Great End of the Church sounds slightly defensive. "Maintenance" implies that divine worship is in doubt, that its continuation is not a certain thing. What is it about divine worship that makes it vulnerable, placing it in need of constant upkeep? The issue is not worship that is "simply divine," of course, but the worship of *God*. Is worship in danger of focusing more on the worshipers than on the One who is to be worshiped? Can worship of God become secondary to reverence for our position, possessions, and possibilities . . . or even our devotion to our congregation?

Preservation of the truth: Our culture is oddly ambivalent about truth, placing unquestioning confidence in scientific truth but resisting religious and moral truth claims. We are more comfortable with multiple truths than with one truth. How are we to understand the universal claims of the gospel in a postmodern world? This foundational purpose of the church not only seems restrictive; it also sounds quite conservative. Should the church look to new and creative approaches to faith and leave preservation to museums and archives? Or is it possible to appreciate that "true novelty is that which does not grow old, despite the passage of time"?[16]

Promotion of social righteousness: How can we understand social justice as a purpose of the church when disagreements about the shape of social justice separate congregations and divide denominations? While all may agree that a just social order is an imperative of the gospel, Alasdair MacIntyre's question confronts us all: "Whose Justice? Which Rationality?"[17] Even when Christians are able to agree on broad social aims, they may disagree sharply on the question of how they are to be "promoted." Means as well as ends are disputed throughout the church. Can the church promote social righteousness, or is the church only able to pursue a variety of disparate strategies for the achievement of often contradictory social ends?

The exhibition of the Kingdom of Heaven to the world: What does the world see when it looks at the church? Will they "know we are Christians by our love," or will they know we are Christians by our sectarian fragmentation and churchly self-concern? Can a divided church display God's new way in the world, or do the church's endless separations damage the credibility of the gospel? Given the world's increasing suspicion of the church, how can each congregation exhibit the reality of God's reign in its place and time?

The sermons in this book do not attempt to provide comprehensive answers to the big questions that are raised for the church by the great purposes set before it. Instead, they do what all faithful preaching does: proclaim God's word in a particular passage of Scripture to a particular people at a particular time. Sermons are not theological lectures or ecclesial instruction manuals, but rather moments in an ongoing conversation between preacher and congregation, a conversation in which God is participant as well as subject. The moments collected here are intended to be part of a conversation with readers and a stimulus to their conversation with others.

Frederick Buechner observes, "Sermons are like dirty jokes; even the best ones are hard to remember."[18] If all that is remembered about these sermons is the possibility and necessity of proclamation that centers preachers and congregations on the grace of the Lord Jesus Christ, the love of God, and the communion of the Holy Spirit—thus calling the church to its reason for being and shaping its mission in the world—the sermons will have fulfilled their own "Great End."

NOTES

1. John Calvin, *Institutes of the Christian Religion* 4.1.9; ed. John T. McNeill, trans. Ford Lewis Battles (Philadelphia: Westminster Press, 1960), 2:1023.

2. David Buttrick, *Homiletic* (Philadelphia: Fortress Press, 1987), 16f.

3. Neil Postman, *Amusing Ourselves to Death* (New York: Viking, 1984), 10.

4. Ibid., 87.

5. Ibid., 121.

6. E. L. Doctorow, *The Waterworks* (New York: Random House, 1994), 143.

7. Douglas John Hall, *Confessing the Faith* (Minneapolis: Fortress Press, 1996), 350.

8. "The Second Helvetic Confession," in *The Constitution of the Presbyterian Church (U.S.A)*, Part I, *The Book of Confessions* (Louisville, KY: Office of the General Assembly, Presbyterian Church (U.S.A.), 2002), 5.004.

9. Karl Barth, *Church Dogmatics*, I/1, trans. G. T. Thompson. (Edinburgh: T.&T. Clark, 1936), 106.

10. Andrew Purves, *Reconstructing Pastoral Theology* (Louisville, KY: Westminster John Knox Press, 2004), 156.

11. *The Confession of 1967: Inclusive Language Text* (Louisville, KY: Office of Theology and Worship, Presbyterian Church (U.S.A.), 2002), 9.49.

12. "The Directory for Worship," in *The Constitution of thePresbyterian Church (U.S.A)*, Part II, *Book of Order* (Louisville, KY: Office of the General Assembly, Presbyterian Church (U.S.A.), 2009), W-2.2007.

13. Karl Barth, "The Need and Promise of Christian Preaching," in *The Word of God and the Word of Man*, trans. Douglas Horton (Glouster, MA: Peter Smith, 1978), 110.

14. *Book of Order*, G-1.0200.

15. See http://www.congregationallifesurvey.

16. Muriel Barbery, *The Elegance of the Hedgehog* (New York: Europa Editions, 2008), 100.

17. Alasdair MacIntyre, *Whose Justice? Which Rationality?* (Notre Dame, IN: University of Notre Dame Press, 1988).

18. Frederick Buechner, *Wishful Thinking: A Theological ABC* (New York: Harper & Row, 1973), 86.

1   The Proclamation of the Gospel for the Salvation of Humankind

Nathanael: Coming Honestly

Jerry Andrews

> *The next day Jesus decided to leave for Galilee. Finding Philip, he said to him, "Follow me."*
>
> *Philip, like Andrew and Peter, was from the town of Bethsaida. Philip found Nathanael and told him, "We have found the one Moses wrote about in the Law, and about whom the prophets also wrote— Jesus of Nazareth, the son of Joseph."*
>
> *"Nazareth! Can anything good come from there?" Nathanael asked.*
>
> *"Come and see," said Philip.*
>
> *When Jesus saw Nathanael approaching, he said of him, "Here truly is an Israelite in whom there is no deceit."*
>
> *"How do you know me?" Nathanael asked.*
>
> *Jesus answered, "I saw you while you were still under the fig tree before Philip called you."*
>
> *Then Nathanael declared, "Rabbi, you are the Son of God; you are the king of Israel."*
>
> *Jesus said, "You believe because I told you I saw you under the fig tree? You will see greater things than that." He then added, "Very truly I tell you, you will see 'heaven open, and the angels of God ascending and descending on' the Son of Man."*
>
> *John 1:43–51 TNIV*

*T*he eighteen verses that open John's Gospel are so full and rich that we are never tempted to think of them as a mere introduction. The "prologue" to John is summative. Like an executive summary the opening eighteen verses consider all the content of the twenty chapters that follow and condense them into one unparalleled statement.

"In the beginning was the Word. . . . And the Word became flesh and dwelt among us, . . . full of grace and truth . . . and we beheld his glory." By the time we leave the Gospel's first eighteen verses we know everything that John wants us to know. If we've fully grasped what is said there, we've got it all.

But this is not how John wants us to learn the good news of Jesus Christ; it is not how John himself learned it. John *beheld* Jesus—he saw him, heard him, touched and was touched by him, loved and was loved by him, walked and talked with him, lived with him. The Word *dwelt* with John!

John shows us the dwelling—what Jesus said, to whom he spoke, what he did, who met him, who touched him and was touched by him, how he lived and died and now lives again. So although the story of Nathanael's calling is only in the first chapter of John's Gospel, everything we need to know is already known because of the prologue. We know who Jesus is from the very start. Nothing will catch us by surprise. Nathanael, however, will experience all of this as something new and startling. And we—those of us who read and hear these words now—if we let God's Word have its full effect on us by God's Spirit . . . *we* will behold Jesus.

John the Baptist recognized Jesus as the Savior of the world on day one. On the next day others begin to come to Jesus one at a time. The conversations between Jesus and these others are brief; from our distance they even seem cryptic. But the short exchanges are pointed, and they make the point.

Andrew is first.

"What do you want?" Jesus asks.

"Rabbi, where are you staying?" Andrew replies.

"Come and you will see," Jesus says.

And then the conversation is over. Andrew and the unnamed second disciple—no doubt John himself—follow Jesus. That's it. The initial conversation is over. Andrew and John will follow and converse with Jesus the remainder of their lives. But this initial conversation is complete. They have found salvation because the Savior has found them.

Simon, Andrew's brother, is next. Andrew says to Simon, "We have found the Messiah," and then brings him to Jesus. Jesus says to Simon, "You are Simon son of John. You will be called Peter." And it's over. Another follower of Jesus; another lifelong disciple.

On the next day, Philip is first. Jesus says, "Follow me." And Philip does. That's it—another believer, another convert.

Then comes Nathanael. Philip seeks Nathanael out. (Are they brothers like Andrew and Peter?) The conversation is a bit longer, but from our vantage point it still seems quite swift and cryptic. And so the conversation needs to be unfolded with special care now in order to be witnessed fully.

Philip says to Nathanael, "We have found the one Moses wrote about in the Law, and about whom the prophets also wrote—Jesus of Nazareth, the son of Joseph." Philip's words are an appeal, an appeal specially designed for the studious Nathanael. Like many in Israel, Nathanael is waiting—perhaps with anticipation, perhaps with cynicism, perhaps alternating between the two, but waiting. Nathanael's waiting is not passive. He reads while he waits; he reads the Scriptures—the Law and the Prophets. Philip knows this about Nathanael and makes the bold proclamation "The one you've been reading about in the ancient script is here!"

You and I know this already. We know it from the prologue to the Gospel: "In the beginning was the Word . . . and the Word became flesh." Philip now knows this, but Nathanael does not. Will Nathanael come to know? How will he know? How will he come to Jesus?

At first, not easily.

He questions Philip; "Nazareth! Can anything good come from Nazareth?" Read "great" for "good" here. It is a legitimate question. Great things and great people normally come from great places like Jerusalem or Egypt. And so when a great person comes from a small place, Scripture makes careful mention of it ("Bethlehem, though you are small, from you shall come the Savior.") Jerusalem, Egypt, and even little Bethlehem all get their due in the predictions of the Prophets . . . but Nazareth receives no mention. Nathanael knows this. It's not simply that Nazareth is small and somewhat inconsequential (everyone mentioned in this story so far lives in or near Nazareth). It's not geography or sociology but the Scriptures that are determinative, and Philip makes his appeal to Nathanael based on the Scriptures . . . where there is no mention of Nazareth. Philip had introduced Jesus, the one long predicted and waited for, as coming from a place that gets no mention at all in the predictions of the Law and the Prophets.

"Nazareth! Can anything great come from a place not even mentioned in the Scriptures?" What is Philip to do with Nathanael's objection? Philip knows the truth about Jesus, but he does not know how to persuade his friend Nathanael. Philip's next move may seem desperate. And maybe it is, but it is also masterful, for it's the same move the Master had made. Repeating Jesus' first words to his first disciples, Philip says simply, "Come and see."

This, John wants us to know, is the perfect invitation: "Come and see." It is an invitation that requires a response and invites the best one. Now it's up to Jesus. The burden of persuasion belongs to Jesus, and he gladly takes the burden. What does Jesus do? Jesus simply presents himself. This is what Jesus has always done:

> He sends his Spirit to convict and convince.
> He speaks his own word of inviting and persuading.

He calls his own disciples and invites his own followers.
He who created the human heart wins it over.
He who constructed the human mind persuades it.

Philip's work is done; Jesus' work begins. As Nathanael approaches, he overhears Jesus say to Philip, "Here is a true Israelite, in whom there is nothing false."

I need to interrupt the narrative at this point to remind you of another one—a narrative that Nathanael knew perfectly well: Isaac and Rebekah had twin boys (like Philip and Nathanael?). They named them "Hairy" (Esau) and "Deceiver" (Jacob). This cannot have worked well for the boys. Comments about Hairy's lack of evolution were inevitable, and the name Deceiver was an obvious handicap when looking for business partners. Remember, ancient Hebrew did not have a separate category of proper nouns with no specific meaning to be used as persons' names. Hebrew names were meant to be descriptive of the person, or prescriptive.

"Deceiver" . . . "Cheater" . . . "False One" . . . Jacob's name was descriptive. He "jacobed" his brother Esau out of his birthright, and then he "jacobed" Esau out of their father's blessing. When this deceit was discovered, Isaac said to the dejected Esau, "Your brother came to me with 'jacob' in his heart." Esau responded, "He is rightly named Jacob, for he has 'jacobed' me two times."

Later God changed Jacob's name. No longer "Cheater," "Deceiver," he was given a new name: "Israel"—"Beloved of God." But his heart was never fully converted, and his own children, learning from their father, "jacobed" him in cruel and consequential ways.

That Jacob was renamed Israel was one of the most powerful stories in Nathanael's Scriptures. That Jacob never fully ceased "jacobing" was a cautionary tale for Nathanael. And so he cultivated the discipline of truth telling, honest action, and living with integrity.

Jesus knows this about Nathanael. When Jesus sees Nathanael coming, he says of him, "Here is truly an Israelite in whom there is no deceit," no "jacob." Nathanael catches the play on words immediately. In that moment, Nathanael receives the highest compliment that Jesus gives in the Gospel. It is the compliment that Nathanael, this careful student of the Scriptures, this honest man, probably most wanted to hear.

But he declines the compliment. Why? Because Nathanael had resolved not only that he would never deceive but also that he would never be deceived. Nathanael had determined to be neither Jacob nor Esau.

And this is where Nathanael's mind is at the moment. His brother Philip has, on the basis of a brief meeting, been persuaded that Jesus is the One and has now proclaimed it to Nathanael. But Nathanael is not so easily convinced. There are Jacobs out there; they are cunning and quick; and they will cheat you out of everything. Has his own brother been deceived? The possibility is on Nathanael's mind. Perhaps as much to save his brother from the deceit as to explore the possibility of the claim being true, he has approached Jesus.

Jesus, it seems, has read his mind and knows what he values. Jesus reads Nathanael as well as Nathanael reads the Scriptures.

"Where did you get to know me?" Nathanael asks. If Jesus truly knows this about him, Nathanael would be impressed. But is it a trick? One cannot be too careful in these matters.

Jesus answers, "I saw you under the fig tree before Philip called you."

The phrase "under the fig tree" is a euphemism for meditating on the things of God—God's ways, God's will, God's word, God. At its best, to be "under the fig tree" is to converse with God, deal with God, and be dealt with by God. This might be agonizing, like Jacob's wrestling with God when his named was changed. In our imagery, Rodin's sculpture "The Thinker," with right elbow on left knee, chin supported by hand, seated and still, is a close equivalent to the image of one seated "under the fig tree."

This is precisely what Nathanael has been doing. (Has he recently been meditating on the Jacob story?) Nathanael's meditating on the things of God was not only a one-time moment—*before Philip called you*—but the basic discipline of his life. Nathanael has been conversing—wrestling—with God.

"I know this about you," says Jesus. "I know what's in your head and what's on your heart. I know what you hope for—the promised One; and what you fear—being *jacobed* by a deceiver. I know this because when you were wrestling with God, Nathanael, you were wrestling with me."

Nathanael did not know what we know: "In the beginning was the Word . . . and the Word was God . . . and the Word became flesh . . . and we beheld his glory . . . glory as of the Father's only Son." Furthermore, you and I know that the faith of the church proclaims that God has always been Father, Son, and Holy Spirit, so that everyone—including every Old Testament character—everyone, when wrestling with God, wrestles with the Son.

While under the fig tree, Nathanael had been wrestling with Jesus. Jesus knows this. John knows this. You and I know this. Now Nathanael knows this.

And he rejoices.

Nathanael replies, "Rabbi, you are the Son of God! You are the King of Israel!" And just like that there is a new disciple of the Master.

But the brief conversation continues with Jesus' longest speech so far in the Gospel—three full sentences:

"Do you believe because I told you that I saw you under the fig tree?" (That is to say, "this is precious little on which to make such a conclusion, Nathanael—very little for one so concerned about being *jacobed*.") "You will see greater things than these. Very truly I tell you that you will see heaven opened and the angels of God ascending and descending upon the Son of Man."

Which brings us back to the story of Jacob. No other narrative in Scripture speaks about angels ascending and descending than the story of Jacob's ladder. Jacob, alone and exhausted, sleeps in the wilderness with a stone for a pillow. He dreams of conversation with God, with the messengers of God climbing up and down a ladder connecting God with humanity. Jacob dreamed this; Nathanael will see it.

Jesus is the Ladder. Human communication with God will take place through him—"ascending and descending upon the Son of Man." All of Nathanael's prayers and all of his wrestlings had been with Jesus, and he will soon see

> the healing of the blind man, and Jesus walking on the water;
> the lame lifted up, and the Son of Man lifted up;
> the wind and waves stilled, and the stone rolled away;
> sinners ascending to God, because God descended to sinners.

When Jacob awoke from his dream he proclaimed, "Surely the Lord is in this place, and I did not know it." Nathanael now makes the same proclamation. The heavens open to Nathanael, and he sees and he knows.

How did all this happen?

No doubt much could be said about Nathanael's preparing himself by his diligent study and honest inquiry. He was found, after all, under the fig tree. The promotion of biblical literacy and sincere exploration of God's ways will always have good effect.

We could say a lot about Nathanael's wrestling with God though he did not know precisely with whom he was conversing. Our neighbors deal with God, and God, with them, even when they do not know it.

We could talk about how Nathanael discovered that he had always been fully known, and how he wanted to be fully loved as he walked and talked with the Savior. Many of us are afraid of being known, lest being known, we would not be loved. Nathanael is both fully known and fully loved. (You don't need to be Nathanael to love that very good news.)

Much could be said about John's purposes in writing his Gospel in a way that shows how initial brief conversations with Jesus lead to faith, and how faith was deepened and sustained in his presence. Sometimes it is amazingly quick and simple how faith begins in earnest.

We could talk a lot about every neighbor of ours and about the fact that no matter how far from God they think themselves to be, they are in unknown conversation with God, who hears every day's dream and every call in the night.

And we could have a full discussion about Jesus gladly bearing the burden of making his own disciples and being the only essential and necessary one in producing faith.

But I want to remind you of the brief conversation between Philip and Nathanael that led to the saving conversation between Jesus and Nathanael. Philip stated his convictions about the Savior to his beloved friend, but then, acknowledging that he could not of himself persuade his brother of what he himself had been persuaded, said simply and beautifully, "Come and see."

This story is about how Nathanael came to Jesus, so it is also a story about Philip. John, in recounting this brief conversation, encourages us to play the role of Philip. John encourages us to invite the Nathanaels in our life, first by stating our convictions about the Savior and then by inviting them to "come and see."

That is the proclamation of the gospel for the salvation of humankind: out of love for neighbors and in obedience to the Lord's command, stating our convictions about the Savior and then graciously inviting them to "come and see."

I imagine that after Philip brought Nathanael to Jesus, he stood a step back and listened in on the conversation between the Savior and Nathanael. Nathanael was not the only one that day who saw the heavens opened and angels of God ascending and descending upon the Son of Man. And Nathanael was not the only one that day that said, "Surely the Lord is in this place."

Amen.

2

Why Did Jesus Die?

Heidi Husted Armstrong

> *Then he handed him over to them to be crucified. So they took Jesus;*
> *and carrying the cross by himself, he went out to what is called The*
> *Place of the Skull, which in Hebrew is called Golgotha. There they*
> *crucified him, and with him two others, one on either side, with Jesus*
> *between them. Pilate also had an inscription written and put on the*
> *cross. It read, "Jesus of Nazareth, the King of the Jews."*
>
> *After this, when Jesus knew that all was now finished, he said (in*
> *order to fulfill the scripture), "I am thirsty." A jar full of sour wine*
> *was standing there. So they put a sponge full of the wine on a branch*
> *of hyssop and held it to his mouth. Then Jesus had received the wine,*
> *he said, "It is finished." Then he bowed his head and gave up his spirit.*
> *John 19:16–19, 28–30*

*P*reachers can be packrats. After twenty-five years of sermonizing I now have file cabinets stuffed with folders on just about every subject imaginable. This is what preachers do: we read like crazy, then clip and file (albeit increasingly electronically!)

A while back I started a file on *The Da Vinci Code*, because when the bestseller started flying off the shelves, some Christians freaked out. Many churches had classes and forums on it, but I think I can give my two-cents worth of analysis in sixty seconds or less:

First, pay attention to the book's cover. In large type it announces *The Da Vinci Code*, followed in really small print by "a novel." Please don't forget: *it's fiction.*

Second, for heaven's sake, don't buy it. *The DaVinci Code* has sold over seventeen million copies! Borrow one.

Third, I read it, and I can say that it *is* a page-turner. But notice: I did not say "good literature." Not even close.

Fourth, it's mediocre literature but even worse theology. It is inaccurate, biased, and misleading. (Although, in my humble opinion, it is probably no worse than the *Left Behind* novels.)

So, fifth, do your homework. Start a file, because frankly, anything that can't stand up to questioning is probably not credible anyway.

And, finally: what about the terrible movie? Honestly, my answer is, *Whatever.* I mean no disrespect to you movie buffs, but movies come, and movies go. People get all worked up about movies, as if it must be true if it's on the big screen. The thing is movies can leave a lot to be desired . . . especially "religious" movies.

Andrea's Question

Do you remember several years ago, just before Easter, how we all packed movie theaters across America to see Mel Gibson's *The Passion of the Christ*? I was struck by something my sister Andrea said to me shortly after she saw *The Passion*. She was one of those who *loved* it. Well, that's not exactly the right word—she was deeply moved by it. As a fairly new believer it brought a lot of things together for her.

And yet after we had talked for quite awhile about how it had affected her, as the conversation was drawing to a close, I'll never forget how Andrea paused and then a bit sheepishly said, "Now, I know I'm supposed to know this . . . *but why did Jesus die?*"

How honest is that? If you've seen the film you know that's one question Mel doesn't really answer. *How* did Jesus die? Well, yes, there's lots of that—maybe too much, especially if you compare the film to our Gospel texts. The Bible is very short on details of Jesus' suffering. But *why* did Jesus die? Sorry, but Gibson pretty much leaves us in the dark. And, truthfully, our text from John's Gospel is not particularly illuminating either; there's very little "how" and zero "why."

So . . . "I know I'm supposed to know this, but why did Jesus die?"

As I talked with my sister that day, I almost went on autopilot. I almost took the easy way out. I almost said, "Well, Jesus died for our sins." Or, "Jesus died to save us." Well, true enough, *but what does that mean?*

So I came clean. I said, "Look, Andrea, I've been a Christian for over thirty years and I still struggle to explain it!" I don't think I'm alone.

A pastor friend of mine accompanied her high school youth group to Mexico to build houses over spring break. The trip took place during Holy Week, and on Maundy Thursday they celebrated the Lord's Supper together. After receiving "the body of Christ broken for you, the blood of Christ poured out for you," one of the students was stymied. "I just don't get it," he said. "Why did Jesus die?" What on earth does the death of this Jewish peasant carpenter on a cross two thousand years ago have to do with anything? The blank look that persisted on that teenager's face was evidence of my friend's valiant but magnificently opaque explanation.

This is one theological question that stymies lots of people, maybe especially Christians, and yes, even pastors. We know we're supposed to know this . . . but why did Jesus die? Why wasn't Jesus just transported directly from earth to heaven? (Hey, it happened before in the Bible, so it could happen again!) Or, why didn't Jesus just die of old age, in his sleep? Why did Jesus have to die, and why did he have to die the way he did?

So I started another file—"Jesus, Death, Why?"—and I've been doing my homework, reading like crazy, clipping, filing . . . and I've discovered a few things.

Scriptural Imagery

The first thing I discovered is that the Gospel writers don't try very hard to answer the question "Why did Jesus die?" Frankly, it made me nervous at first. But commentators tell us it's not that the Gospel writers don't care why Jesus had to die; it's just that they are more intent on *proclaiming* the saving death of Christ than they are *explaining* it!

The other thing I discovered is that when Paul and other New Testament writers *do* address the question "Why did Jesus die?" they do not give one unequivocal answer—evidence that all of them were apparently trying to figure out what it meant, too!

What we see in the New Testament, and later in the early church, is not a single "official" answer to the question "Why did Jesus die?" What we see is the development of *multiple* answers, all of which are true. In Scripture and early church theology, we see different understandings beginning to develop from different perspectives. We see different explanations and diverse metaphors and images, making sense to people in different cultural contexts. What's clear is that no one answer is adequate on its own; no single answer is able to say it all.

Some biblical writers use **financial imagery**. Picture a prison or a slave market, picture captives, people in bondage needing to be liberated. But, of course, freedom is not free. Redemption has a cost. A ransom must be paid. *And that's why Christ died.* His death is the price paid to free humanity from bondage to sin. The Bible uses financial imagery.

Other New Testament writers use **military imagery**. Life is a battlefield where God and the devil are at war, duking it out for possession of God's people. And in Jesus Christ God confronts evil—with nothing, of course, but the weapons of sinlessness and love, not through violence but through his willingness to suffer. At first it appears that God suffers defeat. Jesus *dies*. But then, three days later on Easter morning, there is victory! God triumphs over the power of evil by raising Christ from the dead. Easter's resurrection is God's D-Day. The decisive battle is won. *And that's why Jesus died.*

Still other biblical writers use **legal imagery**. Picture a courtroom where the judge slams the gavel down and pronounces the verdict: Guilty! Those who are guilty of offending God's holiness deserve death. But then the judge takes the punishment upon himself! This is exactly what God does in Jesus Christ: he undergoes our death sentence for us. *This, too, is why Jesus died.*

So we have financial, military, and legal imagery. But perhaps the hardest for us to grasp is **sacrificial imagery**. We have to picture something we have never seen before: ancient worship, which is a far cry from our commanding pipe organ, stately hymns, and peppy praise music! Even the most *CSI–* or *Law and Order*–hardened viewer would likely shudder to see the temple altar filled with bleating animals, their necks outstretched, the flash of sharpened knives, and the sticky spatter and pungent smell of blood—all of which the Bible portrays on the high and holy Day of Atonement.

You can read all about it in Leviticus. When it comes to the meaning of sacrifice, one commentator describes Leviticus as "a primer with big pictures and big print." Chapter 16 gives the basics: the temple is filled with guilty people who are estranged from God, needing forgiveness. The priest offers a sacrifice as a symbol of their corporate remorse as a substitute. This is how sacrifice works: a life for a life. Blood is shed because life is in the blood (Lev. 17:11, 14). And the result is forgiveness, reconciliation, atonement— "at-one-ment"—because relationship with God is restored.

But that's not all, because there is another sacrifice on the Day of Atonement. There is a second goat, the "scapegoat," that is symbolically loaded up with all the sins of the people and then sent away, forgotten. This is also what God does. God not only forgives; God also forgets! Sin is now out of sight, out of mind.

But in the New Testament things get even better, because now Jesus is not only priest; he is also the sacrifice. *Jesus* is the substitute, atoning for human sin *once and for all*. The Letter to the Hebrews says, "Without the shedding of blood there is no forgiveness of sins" But it also says, "if the blood of goats . . . sanctifies those who have been defiled . . . *how much more* will the blood of Christ, who . . . offered himself without blemish to God, purify our conscience . . . to worship the living God!" (Heb. 9:13–14, 22). Jesus is our sacrifice, our substitute. Jesus is the scapegoat who takes away the sins of the world. *And that's why Jesus died.*

Still, Why Does It Take All This?

So there are a variety of explanations, multiple images, for why Jesus died. Yet I think if we're honest, we still wonder, *Does it really take all this?* I mean, if God is God, and God can do whatever God wants (which is what it means to be God; it's in the job description!) then can't God just forgive and forget without all this blood-and-death stuff?

This is not to minimize sin. Sin is a big deal. Thumbing our noses at the Creator, telling the Almighty to get lost, is a big deal. The result—broken relationships with God, with one another, with all of creation—is a huge deal. I'll give you that. But if God is God, can't God just choose to *say,* "I forgive you," and be done with it?

So you see the question is still lurking: Why did Jesus *have* to die?

Well, Scottish theologian and preacher Donald Baillie puts it this way. Suppose you hurt somebody, somebody you love. (I know this is a stretch, but stay with me here!) And so you say to that person, "I am so sorry I hurt you; I feel really bad about it." And then that person says, "Well, it's OK. It's no big deal. Why don't we just forget it." *Is that really forgiveness?*

What is the person really saying? Isn't that person actually saying something closer to "I don't really care enough about you to be bothered by anything you say or do. You're not that important to me"? So what happens is, you end up sitting there nursing the pain of your guilt when in fact what you really need is that person to help you deal with it, to help you clean the slate so that you can start fresh and move on. In other words, as Baillie so eloquently puts it,

> Good-natured indulgence and casual acceptance are not forgiveness and love, but [in reality they are] an expression of indifference and sometimes [even] hostility. [In fact] real love and forgiveness mean caring enough to be hurt, caring enough to put ourselves in [an]other's shoes and sharing their guilt as if it were our own. Real love and forgiveness are costly—not just in the sense that the guilty party must squeeze them out of the injured party but in the sense that the injured party genuinely sympathizes with the guilty and shares [their] pain.

And this is what God does!

Relational Imagery

So, Andrea, why did Jesus die? Jesus died because God cares for us too much to say, "Oh, it doesn't really matter; let's just forget it." God does not flippantly dismiss our sin and guilt—because it *does* matter.

Jesus died because words alone don't cut it; because actions speak louder than words. In Jesus' death God acts to demonstrate that God's love and forgiveness are genuine.

Jesus died because when we thumb our noses at God, when we tell God and others in our lives to "get lost"—resulting in separation, loneliness, and alienation—God deliberately stands *with* us. God *won't* "get lost."

Donald Baillie continues, "In the cross God says to us, 'Yes, it is true. You *have* hurt and offended me. But I still love you.'" In fact, God says, I love you so much "I will make your guilt and its consequences my own." I love you so much "I will suffer with you—[and] *for* you—to make things right between us again."

In other words, for us to understand why Christ died it takes **relational imagery**. And, what's more, when we begin to employ this relational imagery we begin to understand that it is God's *love* that motivates Christ death, not God's *anger*.

How often do we hear people say that the Son dies on the cross to appease the Father's anger? Of course, they still try to maintain that God is loving, but if you ask me that feels a little like having the owner of a dog who is barking, growling, and straining at its leash say, "Don't worry, he doesn't bite." Yeah, right! I mean, have you ever felt that sometimes people make it sound like what Jesus came to save us from was . . . *God!*

The name of our church is Trinity Presbyterian, but for many people the Trinity is shorthand for some unexplainable, esoteric theology. So here's some down-to-earth, accessible Trinitarian theology for you today: two thousand years ago the Trinity—Father, Son, and Holy Spirit—were *not* having a big fight on Calvary! The Father and Son were not battling it out on the cross with the Spirit trying to referee, or maybe just trying to stay out of the way and not get in trouble.

It is not God versus Jesus on the cross, with the Spirit playing Switzerland. No, on the cross it's *all* of God against *sin*; it's *all* of God *for* humanity. God is not the problem; *sin* is the problem. *Those are the arms of God stretched wide in a loving embrace from the cross.*

And that's why Jesus died!

We Presbyterians believe that one of the reasons the church exists is for "the proclamation of the gospel for the salvation of humankind" (it's actually the first thing on the list of the church's purposes). I believe we proclaim the good news of the saving death of Jesus Christ most compellingly when we stay with this *relational* imagery because we are called not only to proclaim the cross but also to live it—to demonstrate love, forgiveness, and hope; to put ourselves in another's shoes; to suffer with others. We are called to express God's love as Jesus did—by ministering in weakness, vulnerability, and suffering love; by caring enough to be hurt; by letting our hearts be broken.

Could it be that the greatest influence in inviting others to become followers of Christ is the *lifestyle* of Christians—a lifestyle marked by authenticity, transparency, love, forgiveness? And isn't *that* why Jesus died . . . not merely to provide us with a ticket to heaven someday but to be the key to a new kind of existence now, an existence that proclaims the gospel of salvation with our very lives! Surely this is some of what Jesus means when he says, "As the Father sent me, so I send you" (John 20:21). For followers of Jesus, *life is cruciform.* That too is why Jesus died—that we might *live* for him!

By the power of God who is at work within us, thanks be to God! Amen.

ACKNOWLEDGMENTS

My file on "Jesus, Death, Why?" is filled with notes from the following: William Placher, *Jesus the Savior: The Meaning of Jesus Christ for Christian Faith* (Louisville, KY: Westminster John Knox Press, 2001), 111–56; Shirley Guthrie, *Christian Doctrine,* rev. ed. (Louisville, KY: Westminster John Knox Press, 1994), 250–69; Daniel Migliore, *Faith Seeking Understanding: An Introduction to Christian Theology* (Grand Rapids: Wm. B. Eerdmans Publishing Co. 1991), 151–56; and Joel B. Green and Mark D. Baker, *Recovering the Scandal of the Cross: Atonement in New Testament and Contemporary Contexts,* (Downers Grove, IL: InterVarsity Press, 2000).

The quote about sacrifice in Leviticus is taken from Walter Kaiser, *New Interpreter's Bible,* vol. 1, *Genesis to Leviticus* (Nashville: Abingdon, 1994).

I draw heavily for my understanding of relational imagery from Donald Baillie's analogy in *God Was In Christ,* 171ff., quoted by Guthrie, *Christian Doctrine,* 260.

Presbyterian Church (U.S.A.), *The Constitution of the Presbyterian Church (U.S.A.),* Part II, *Book of Order* (Louisville, KY: Office of the General Assembly, 1999), G-1.0200.

3

Then Who Can Be Saved?

Theodore J. Wardlaw

As [Jesus] was setting out on a journey, a man ran up and knelt before him, and asked him, "Good Teacher, what must I do to inherit eternal life?" Jesus said to him, "Why do you call me good? No one is good but God alone. You know the commandments: 'You shall not murder; You shall not commit adultery; You shall not steal; You shall not bear false witness; You shall not defraud; Honor your father and mother.'" He said to him, "Teacher, I have kept all these since my youth." Jesus, looking at him, loved him and said, "You lack one thing; go, sell what you own, and give the money to the poor, and you will have treasure in heaven; then come, follow me." When he heard this, he was shocked and went away grieving, for he had many possessions.

Then Jesus looked around and said to his disciples, "How hard it will be for those who have wealth to enter the kingdom of God!" And the disciples were perplexed at these words. But Jesus said to them again, "Children, how hard it is to enter the kingdom of God! It is easier for a camel to go through the eye of a needle than for someone who is rich to enter the kingdom of God." They were greatly astounded and said to one another, "Then who can be saved?" Jesus looked at them and said, "For mortals it is impossible, but not for God; for God all things are possible."

Peter began to say to him, "Look, we have left everything and followed you." Jesus said, "Truly I tell you, there is no one who has left house or brothers or sisters or mother or father or children or fields, for my sake and for the sake of the good news, who will not receive a hundredfold now in this age—houses, brothers and sisters, mothers and children, and fields with persecutions—and in the age to come eternal life. But many who are first will be last, and the last will be first."

Mark 10:17–31

*T*he very first of the "Great Ends of the Church" is a mouthful: "the Proclamation of the Gospel for the Salvation of Humankind." Try saying that three
times fast. Way back near the beginning of the twentieth century, good people
set about trying to summarize and focus how the church should understand
its core mission. This led, of course, to the development of the "Great Ends
of the Church," and the first objective laid out—wordy as it was—was "the
Proclamation of the Gospel for the Salvation of Humankind." Perhaps by
today's standards there's a sepia-toned quaintness to this turn-of-a-century-
ago value. If we could get away with it, we might shorten this value—make
it snappier. Something like, "Good News 'R Us."

But we could hardly improve upon the intent of this statement. Those
faithful people who thought it into being were convinced that a church could
not really be a church without starting with this proclamation of the gospel.
They were right, I think. Turn to practically any page of Scripture, and you
will see evidence of the people of God proclaiming the goodness of God. For
example, the psalmist says,

> The LORD is my light and my salvation;
>   whom shall I fear?
> The LORD is the stronghold of my life;
> of whom shall I be afraid?

Moses and the Israelites, having outrun the pursuing Egyptians, and now
resting there on the far banks of the sea, sang in celebration:

> "Who is like you, O LORD, among the gods?
>   Who is like you, majestic in holiness,
> awesome in splendor, doing wonders?
> . . . .
> In your steadfast love you led the people whom you redeemed;
>   you guided them by your strength to your holy abode.
> . . . .
> You brought them in and planted them on the mountain of your own
>   possession,
> . . . .
> the sanctuary, O LORD, that your hands have established."

The prophet Isaiah says,

> O LORD, you are my God;
> I will exalt you, I will praise your name;
> for you have done wonderful things,
> plans formed of old, faithful and sure.

And the prophet Amos admonishes, "Come, let us return to the Lord; for it is God who has torn, and God will heal us; God has struck down, and God will bind us up…" Everywhere you look in Scripture, although the nuances may differ, people are proclaiming the greatness of God! The apostle Paul proclaims, "God was in Christ, reconciling the world to God . . . and entrusting to us the message of reconciliation" And John, in the Revelation of John, says,

> "See, the home of God is among mortals.
> God will dwell with them as their God;
> they will be God's peoples, and God will be with them."

You can hardly turn a page in Scripture without brushing up against people who have heard "the proclamation of the gospel for the salvation of humankind." But hearing it is one thing; taking part in its awesome power is another.

I'm thinking about the man in our text from Mark's Gospel. We've come to know him as "the rich young ruler," even though Mark doesn't describe him that way. It amazes me, really, that over time we've set this man up with such a title. Maybe we had to do it in order to build in some comfortable distance between him and ourselves, because there's something about him—can you see it?—that makes us uncomfortable. That title gets in the way of his ability to connect with us, I think; so let's get rid of the title. The man isn't a ruler, and he isn't necessarily young.

But he is rich—he's a lot like many of us. And not just rich. He's also respectable; he's successful; he comes with all of the right credentials. He has a long string of Sunday-school medals hanging from his lapel, showing twenty years of perfect attendance. He's been on the finance committee for years; he's chaired the stewardship campaign; he's been on city council; he's been vice president of the PTA; he's worked hard. In his office, all the framed awards and diplomas and citations have to share space with the pictures of his wife and kids. At home—which, by the way, is in a desirable part of town—he makes time to help with the chores and get involved with the neighborhood issues. He pays the civic rent. Truth to tell, he's a lot like we are.

But all the same, there's something about him, isn't there? There's something we can't quite put our finger on. It's not his achievement, because we certainly value achievement. He's a lot like we are. And it's not the way he runs up to Jesus all full of urgency—kneeling there and flattering him and asking him a deep question about how to inherit eternal life. That just shows he's got chutzpah. He's a lot like we are!

It's not his appearance. It's not his background. It's not any of that. In fact, it's nothing that we can see. I think it's something that we suspect is lurking beneath what we can see. We wonder what this man is concealing, because look at him! He's too perfect! What personal secrets are there that haven't reached the full light of day? What betrayals has he been able to hide? What resentments, or jealousies, or occasions for hurt, or desires, or falsehoods have thus far escaped disclosure? There's something about this man that isn't so handsomely packaged, that isn't so neatly scripted, that isn't yet on the table in the full light of day so that we would have a clearer picture of just exactly who he really is. Because, after all . . . he's a lot like we are.

He's a lot like we are. Could it be that this, above all else, is what we don't like about him? God knows we don't like being vulnerable, exposed. So we learn to practice the art of concealment. We even learn, sometimes, to believe about ourselves the things we have maneuvered others into believing about us. So for all sorts of reasons each of us fear—more, perhaps, than anything else—the tragedy of exposure; of being seen and known for who we really are.

I often have bad Saturday-night dreams about Sunday-morning worship. I've had them on many Saturday nights across twenty-three years of parish ministry; and even though for the past seven years my ministry has taken the form of a seminary presidency, I still have these Saturday-night dreams.

Sometimes I dream that the choir is coming out of the sacristy and into the church, and I'm still back there trying to get my robe buttoned up. Or maybe I'm ransacking my office trying to find my sermon. Then, suddenly—wait!—I realize that somehow I forgot to write a sermon. Sometimes in my dreams, I stand in the pulpit, and I open my mouth, and I discover that I can't talk. And sometimes, I can make sounds, but they're not words—it's just noisy croaking, as if I'm a frog. Once or twice on a Saturday night, I've dreamed that I came in on time and stepped into the pulpit, and my text was there, and I was able to speak—all of that was just right. But then, to my horror, I look down and notice that not only is my robe not on—I don't have anything on!

My wife, who is a psychologist, tells me that those are anxiety dreams, anxiety over the fear of exposure, the fear of being discovered, the fear of being stripped naked. What would people think of me, how could they listen to me preach, if they could get beneath the externals to the heart of who I am? That's the anxiety: to be seen as you really are. Who in their right mind wants that?

As a seminary student, I sometimes attended a grand old church on Sunday mornings. It was a downtown church, rather large in membership. I enjoyed the pastor's preaching, the beautiful music, the stained-glass windows, the stately architecture, and the church's mission in the middle of that city. This church had an antebellum sanctuary building in the Greek-revival style, with a high, flat ceiling. In the middle of that ceiling was a large, perfect triangle—a symbol of the Trinity—and in the middle was painted what the Christian church throughout its history has chosen as a symbol for God. It was a single unblinking eye—the eye of God that stared down on all of the people every Sunday from that high vantage point, penetrating the hearts of all of us. It intimidated me, to be honest, for I feared what that eye might see within me. I understood how the author of the Epistle to the Hebrews could write, "There is nothing in creation that can hide from Him; everything lies naked and exposed to the eyes of One with whom we have to reckon."

That doesn't sound much like the proclamation of the gospel, does it? But here's some gospel. Over time, I put it together: the eye of God—majestic and cosmic and high and unreachable and untouchable and all-seeing—has also looked at us from the face of One who was, himself, a lot like we are. And that makes all the difference in the world.

Kneeling in the dust before Jesus, with his briefcase and his umbrella neatly stowed away next to him, the man trotted out all of his credentials, name-dropped all of his associations, did everything except lick Jesus' feet. And what happened next is easily overlooked, because the narrative moves quickly at this point. But don't miss it! Mark writes, "Jesus, looking at him, loved him." Not "liked him," not "was intrigued by him," not "found him interesting." *Loved him*! It's more than admiration or respect or sentimentality. It is the gut-wrenching concern that one has for a loved one about to take his or her own life. All that's important in such a moment is to point that one desperately toward the best reason in all the world to live!

Jesus saw everything, of course—the smugness, the self-righteous confidence, the obsequiousness, everything. He saw the disappointments, the half-forgotten shame, the private anguish that had provoked the man's question in the first place, everything! Jesus, looking at everything about him, nonetheless . . . *loved* him! How remarkable it is, to be seen like that by the eye of God and still be loved.

The man didn't want to hear what Jesus said next. And after he went sadly away, Jesus had some very tough things to say about how hard it is to cast aside the perfect attendance pins and the diplomas and the citations and the bonuses and all the other dependencies that keep us from standing bare before the God who gives. Lord knows, we all struggle with that. It's not just our money and our privilege that makes the struggle so hard. It's anything! It's the futility, the utter impossibility of earning our inheritance. We may as well try to earn our genetic makeup, or to choose our parents, or to earn the air we breathe. You can't earn something that's free! It's impossible—just as impossible as the assignment Jesus had given that man.

But I can't help wondering if it was not only this one man Jesus was thinking of when he added, "But for God all things are possible." Imagine that! All things are possible for God! The rich man was possible for God . . . and you and I are possible for God! *All* things!

The vision that sees us with unblinking eye, stripping us naked and seeing what we can hardly bear to see, is a loving vision! "Jesus, looking at him, loved him. . . ." Such a vision desires, above all else, to transform us and to give us something of that same vision to see with our own eyes. The vision that apprehends us also sears right through us, casting light into all of our shadowy places, scorching away all that is ugly to see, even burning through those leaded encasements in which we hide our hearts. Seeing all of that, God loves us.

Then, as we are seen, and as we come to understand the loving gaze under which we all live and move and have our being, we find that we too are granted a measure of such vision. Even we are able to see the world and all of life as an arena in which holy things happen. We are able to see each other not as objects to be competed with and manipulated but as sisters and brothers.

I love the way C. S. Lewis put it: "There are no ordinary people," he said. "You have never talked with a mere mortal . . . it is immortals whom we joke with, work with, marry, snub, and exploit. . . . Next to the Blessed Sacrament itself, your neighbor is the holiest object presented to your senses. And holy in almost the same way, for in him or her . . . Christ is truly hidden."

"Jesus, looking at him, loved him," and Jesus, looking at us, loves us. And when Jesus looks at the whole world, he loves it, too. All of this is remarkable because, as people and as a world, we are seldom all that lovely. And what is more, we are full of ourselves, not even sure we need God's love.

The late William F. Buckley, the often exasperating but also magnetic conservative journalist and pundit, once wrote a book on why he was a Christian. In his book he took note of how, in so many instances, our culture betrays how embarrassed we are by God. He noted that at his own prep school, Millbrook, they stopped having Christmas services and began referring to them instead as "candlelight services." In his own wicked fashion, Buckley then reflected: "The Spiritual Life Committee at Millbrook treats the word 'Christmas' as Victorians treated the word 'syphilis,' though more Victorians contracted syphilis, one supposes, than at this rate, Millbrook students contract Christianity." That's an accurate picture, I think, of what is unlovely about our world.

But it's not the whole story. It's only half of the story.

I'm told that when someone enters Coventry Cathedral in England, to go to evensong or some other service of worship, it's possible to pick up a copy of a service booklet that bears these words across the top: "You are coming in on a conversation which began long before you were born and will continue long after you are dead." A conversation that's been going on in our world since the very beginning—I love the way that is put. It is the same conversation that lies at the root of everything we do in church—the things we discuss in church school, the music we teach our children, the money and time and energy we give back to God through the act of stewardship, the people who touch us and whom we try to touch in our various ministries. The whole picture of who we are in the sight of God and how we strive to see the world with that same kind of vision are all part of that ongoing conversation.

And what's that conversation about, for God's sake, if not "the proclamation of the gospel for the salvation of humankind"?

ACKNOWLEDGMENTS

C. S. Lewis, *The Weight of Glory* (New York: HarperOne, 2001).

William F. Buckley, *Nearer My God: An Autobiography of Faith* (Fort Washington, PA: Harvest Books, 1998).

I am grateful to my friend, Dean Thompson, who mentioned the Coventry Cathedral service book in his introduction to the October 1997 issue of *Interpretation.*

4

The Dogma in the Drama

K. Nicholas Yoda

> *If I proclaim the gospel, this gives me no ground for boasting, for an obligation is laid on me, and woe to me if I do not proclaim the gospel! For if I do this of my own will, I have a reward; but if not of my own will, I am entrusted with a commission. What then is my reward? Just this: that in my proclamation I may make the gospel free of charge, so as not to make full use of my rights in the gospel.*
>
> *1 Cor. 9:16–18*

John Newton was born in London, England, in 1725, the son of John Newton Sr., a shipmaster in the Mediterranean service, and Elizabeth Newton, a Nonconformist Christian. His early years were turbulent as he witnessed his mother's passing from tuberculosis at the age of six, spent a few years at a boarding school, and then went to sea with his father at the age of eleven. He made a total of six voyages until the elder Newton retired in 1742.

Newton's father intended for him to take up a position as a slave master at a sugar plantation in Jamaica, but instead young Newton began sailing on a slave ship. This resulted in a life of immorality that would lead him to describe himself later as "an infidel and libertine." All of this changed in 1748 while he was sailing back to England aboard the merchant ship *The Greyhound*. One night, as the ship encountered a severe storm and almost sank, Newton met the Devil. He awoke in the middle of the night and called out to God as the ship filled with water. It was this experience that Newton later marked as the beginning of his conversion to evangelical Christianity.

John Newton would go on to write great hymns, most notably *Amazing Grace*; to stand by the side of William Wilberforce in his quest to eradicate the slave trade in the British Empire; and to proclaim the gospel of Jesus Christ for the salvation of humankind for decades in the Church of England. In one particular sermon, he stepped into the pulpit, cleared his throat, and began with the following words: "I count it my honor and happiness that I preach to a free people who have their Bibles in their hands. I appeal—I entreat—I charge you to receive nothing upon my word any further than I can prove it from the Word of God. And bring every preacher and every sermon that you hear to the same standard."

"And bring every preacher and every sermon that you hear to the same standard." That statement should make any teacher and preacher of God's word nervous. It makes me nervous. Maybe this is why James, the brother of Jesus, writes in his letter to the twelve tribes of Israel in the Dispersion (Jewish Christians outside of Palestine), "Let not many of you become teachers, my brethren, knowing that as such we will incur a stricter judgment." Preachers and teachers need to be reminded of the prayer that the great evangelist Billy Graham is rumored to say each morning, "Please Lord, do not let me embarrass you today."

"And bring every preacher and every sermon that you hear to the same standard." To parse this statement in the context of the rest of the monologue by Newton, two foundational marks can be noted. First, there is a reference point from which all sermons must flow to and from. There is a plumb line of truth to which all teachings can be compared. That point of reference—that plumb line—is, of course, the Bible, the Holy Scriptures, the Word of God. And no sermon or teaching based on this Word should be an adventure in missing the point. Scottish Preacher Alistair Begg put it this way: "In preaching, glory must flow to and from God because anything less is not being truthful to the word properly exposited." It can be summed up properly in a fortune that I recently found in a cookie after eating Chinese food at my in-laws that reads, "Integrity is the essence of everything successful." Every sermon and teaching must be of the same essence as the Bible to hold on to its integrity and be a faithful exposition.

The second mark is that preachers/teachers have a specific function with certain boundaries set to hold them accountable. The Bible expositor is supposed to be taking the Word of God and opening up what might be closed, making plain what might be obscure, unraveling what is noted, and unfolding what is tightly packed. It was Robert Wall of Seattle Pacific University who stated, "We have to have pastors invested in the theological formation of their congregations or we are lost as a church." A preacher in the pulpit is like a surgeon with a scalpel. His tool can be used properly to save, or in its misuse it can destroy. If preachers/teachers are doing anything contrary to the job of a Bible expositor, and if they do not undertake the theological formation of their congregations with the utmost discernment, then by no means are we ever to look at their labors as spiritual gifts.

Listen again to Alistair Begg:

As long as ministers in the pulpit trim their faith and their sermons to the pervading theological wind, as long as we dilute the hard sayings of Jesus so as to make them seeker friendly, as long as we are prepared to blend with the culture, to laugh at its jokes, to share in its immorality, in short, as long as we choose to live with compromise, we need not fear any possibility of slander, imprisonment and death. We can frankly just relax. But, if we are prepared in our pulpits first to lead our people in a strong stand in a world of pluralism concerning the exclusivity of the claims of Christ, if we are prepared in our pulpits to lead our people in a dirty world, to take a strong stand concerning the purity that is represented in following Christ, if we are prepared in our pulpits to take a strong stand in leading our people concerning the sufficiency and authority of the Scriptures, then we may want to keep Christ and His Word revealed on Scripture handy.

The Italian word *pastore* is translated as "shepherd." A pastor's calling is to properly shepherd the flock by the Word of God found in the Scriptures. Not everyone standing behind a pulpit is called by God. Not all who shows up with Bible in hand and a message upon their lips has God's intentions and the best interest of the people at heart. And in the context of the church, says Alistair Begg, "A congregation will often take on the primary emphasis of the one teaching the Bible and when truth is shunned and error is embraced, you will find ungodliness and bitter division."

"Let not many of you become teachers, my brethren, knowing that as such we will incur a stricter judgment." Although James probably wrote this statement a decade before Paul penned his first letter to the church in Corinth, it is a logical inference that they are of the same mind and heart, for we read in 1 Corinthians 9:16–18,

If I proclaim the gospel, this gives me no ground for boasting, for an obligation is laid on me; and woe to me if I do not proclaim the gospel! For if I do this of my own will, I have a reward; but if not of my own will, I am entrusted with a commission. What then is my reward? Just this: that in my proclamation I may make the gospel free of charge, so as not to make full use of my rights in the gospel.

Paul is transparent in his intention to remain congruent with the plumb line of the truth of the gospel and be one who exposits nothing less than that which has been entrusted to him. Paul knew that clarity in his proclamation was of the utmost importance because of the nature of Corinth. There had to be a spirit of boldness tempered by humility so as to speak words of truth that were staggering to the ears of men and women.

Paul's words must be understood in their proper context. Ancient Corinth was an expansive city—a mighty city—a crossroads of commercial enterprise drawing persons from all over the Roman world. Ancient Corinth was a city of people in the know—cosmopolitan, skeptical, sophisticated, and cynical. Ancient Corinth was a city filled with disillusionment, and it may have been a minor miracle that a church was planted there in the first place. For some reason, Paul, who was called by God to preach and teach the salvific message of Jesus Christ, loved the city of Corinth and remained there a long time, perhaps his longest stay in an itinerant lifestyle of missionary journeys.

Paul, like the city of Corinth, was also a convergence of cultures. Born a Hebrew, he became a Roman citizen and received training in a Greek city. From the Hebrews, Paul learned the moral categories of life—the light in the darkness. From the Romans, Paul learned the legal categories of life—the glory of the empire. From the Greeks, Paul learned the philosophical categories of life—the knowledge of the academy. And as a convinced follower of Jesus Christ, Paul wove what he had learned from these three distinct cultures with the reality of the incarnation into a proclamation for which he would eventually die. Paul does the task of theology, which is to clarify and preserve the faith in God who caused the light to shine out of darkness and has caused, according to Dr. Ravi Zacharias, "His light to shine in our hearts to give us the *light* of the *knowledge* of the *glory* of God in the face of Christ Jesus our Lord."

How did ancient Corinth embrace Paul and his message? They diminished him. They attacked his voice, saying it was weak. They attacked his appearance, saying it was not attractive. They attacked his courage, saying that his writings were passionate yet his message in the flesh was cowardly. And finally they attacked his motive, saying all was done for personal gain. But in the midst of all of this, Paul knew that as a teacher and preacher of the gospel message he would be judged on three important factors: the content of his teaching, the conduct of his life, and the motive of his message. Paul was well aware that a certain blindness to the gospel was already present in Corinth, and because he is called to preach and teach that gospel, it could not be a case of the blind leading the blind. The message that Paul preached was not meant to be an appeal to the felt needs of the community, telling them they are great, exalting their self-esteem, and soothing their consciences. This would be disastrous and make Paul a very dangerous man. It has been said that the teacher who is self-deceived is the most dangerous of teachers. Paul would be among this crowd had he not preached the Word of God with integrity and fidelity.

If I proclaim the gospel, this gives me no ground for boasting, for an obligation is laid on me; and woe to me if I do not proclaim the gospel! For if

I do this of my own will, I have a reward; but if not of my own will, I am entrusted with a commission. What then is my reward? Just this: that in my proclamation I may make the gospel free of charge, so as not to make full use of my rights in the gospel.

When the gospel is proclaimed for the salvation of humankind, every preacher and every sermon should be held to the highest standards—that of John Newton and James and Paul as well as of God. The Bible is not given to us to satisfy our curiosity, but it has been given to us in order that our lives may be changed by it. The Bible is a book about Jesus. Alex Matea states, "In the Old Testament, He is predicted. In the Gospels, He is revealed. In the Acts, He is preached. In the Epistles, He is explained. In the Revelation, He is expected." There is no question about this. There is an exclamation point, but not a question mark.

People will give their lives to the truth that is followed by an exclamation point. They will not give their lives over to a question mark. For once the protest runs out, according to Kevin DeYoung and Ted Kluck, "There will be no exclamation point, and all that's left will be ethical intentions. There will be no great vision of God, no urgent proclamation of salvation, no eternal judgment or reward at stake, just a call to live rightly and love one another. This message will sell on *Oprah*, *Larry King*, and at the Oscars, but it won't sustain and propel a gospel-driven church, because it isn't the gospel." The church of Jesus Christ is supposed to be about the Father, Son, and Holy Spirit; the death and resurrection of Jesus; his atonement for our sins; the promise of eternal life; and the threat of coming judgment. We must hold on to the reality that we have to believe and live and proclaim this amazing story with all its glorious doctrinal propositions.

In the words of Dorothy Sayers, "It is the dogma that is the drama. Not beautiful phrases, nor comforting sentiment, nor vague aspirations to loving kindness and uplift, nor the promise of something nice after death—but the terrifying assertion that the same God who made the world lived in the world and passed through the grave and gate of death. Show that to the heathen and they may not believe it; but at least they may realize that here is something that a man might be glad to believe."

Amen.

ACKNOWLEDGMENTS:

Kevin DeYoung and Ted Kluck, *Why We're Not Emergent (By Two Guys Who Should Be)* (Chicago, IL: Moody Publishers, 2008), 127.

Dorothy Sayers, *Creed or Chaos? Why Christians Must Choose Either Dogma or Disaster (Or, Why it Really Does Matter What You Believe)* (Manchester, NH: Sophia Institute Press, 1999), 25.

2

The Shelter, Nurture, and Spiritual Fellowship of the Children of God

5

Starting at the Ends

Christine Chakoian

> *When he returned to Capernaum after some days, it was reported that he was at home. So many gathered around that there was no longer room for them, not even in front of the door; and he was speaking the word to them. Then some people came, bringing to him a paralyzed man, carried by four of them. And when they could not bring him to Jesus because of the crowd, they removed the roof above him; and after having dug through it, they let down the mat on which the paralytic lay. When Jesus saw their faith, he said to the paralytic, "Son, your sins are forgiven." Now some of the scribes were sitting there, questioning in their hearts, "Why does this fellow speak this way? It is blasphemy! Who can forgive sins but God alone?" At once Jesus perceived in his spirit that they were discussing these questions among themselves; and he said to them. "Why do you raise such questions in your hearts? Which is easier, to say to the paralytic, 'Your sins are forgiven,' or to say, 'Stand up and take your mat and walk'? But so that you may know that the Son of Man has authority on earth to forgive sins"—he said to the paralytic—"I say to you, stand up, take your mat and go to your home." And he stood up, and immediately took the mat and went out before all of them; so that they were all amazed and glorified God, saying, "We have never seen anything like this!"*
>
> *Mark 2:1–12*

*T*here is a hunger abroad in our time," writes Marjorie Thompson in her lovely book *Soul Feast*:

> There is a hunger abroad in our time, haunting lives and hearts. Like an empty stomach aching beneath the sleek coat of a seemingly well-fed culture, it reveals that something is missing from the diet of our rational, secular, and affluent culture.

If you think that's hyperbole, walk into any Barnes & Noble and browse the shelves of self-help and spirituality books. Lutheran pastor Rick Barger suggests that even the proximity of these two departments "speaks volumes about the spiritual hunger of our culture." Indeed, Barger says, "Many come into a *worship* service not sure of what they want but know that they need 'something.'"

What is it that you need? For what are you hungry? Most of us come to worship hungry for something. Maybe it's a hunger for healing—the mending of strained relationships—or the restoration of bodies broken by physical or mental illness, or a hunger for meaning, a longing for something more than a fabulous culture and gorgeous vacations provide. Maybe it's a hunger to feel adequate and affirmed, or forgiven for being a jerk, or simply a yearning to be comforted after a tough week in the trenches. Perhaps it's a hunger for rest, for reprieve from our busy schedules, the tyranny of cell phones and e-mail, and the nagging sense of never having or being "enough."

My guess is most of us come here hungry for something, even if we cannot name it.The question is, How shall we fill that hunger? "There is no shortage of restaurants offering to fill our emptiness," notes Joe Small of our denomination's Office of Theology and Worship. "From the fast food of New Age crystals and pyramids to the five-star cuisine of ancient Asian religions, the menus are many and varied. Is the church just one more café on restaurant row?"

"Am I getting what I want out of church?" is the wrong question for us to ask. Not because our needs don't matter but because all of the congregational programs and good causes in the world cannot meet those needs. If we come to church as consumers in a store, we will be disappointed.

Instead, God invites us to come here expecting more . . . to come expecting a real relationship with God. To come, trusting that the Lord can and will feed our deepest hungers. To come, as the prophet Isaiah writes, expecting that "the Lord will guide you continually, and satisfy your needs in parched places." To come, and find within these walls nothing less than "the shelter, nurture, and spiritual fellowship of the children of God."

"Our hearts are restless until they find their rest in Thee," St. Augustine prayed. When we are willing to let God's house become more than a café at which we come to graze—when we let it be our "heart's true home"—then we will find rest for our souls.

Writer Ann Lamott tells the story a little girl of seven who got lost one day:

> The little girl ran up and down the streets of the big town where they lived, but she couldn't find a single landmark. She was very frightened. Finally a policeman stopped to help her. He put her in the passenger seat of his car,

and they drove around until she finally saw her church. She pointed it out to the policeman, and then she told him firmly, "You could let me out now. This is my church, and I can always find my way home from here."

This, Lamott says, is how she feels about her church: "Because no matter how bad I am feeling, how lost or lonely or frightened, when I see the faces of the people at my church, and hear their tawny voices, I can always find my way home." It's so easy to get lost these days—to get lost in the arbitrary competition for status, lost in the artificial requirements of beauty, lost in the empty promises of money, lost in the frenetic busy-ness of our postmodern pace. It's so easy to get lost these days . . . it's a wonder we find our way home at all.

But to me, our spiritual home is much more than just a place of safety. Our spiritual home is where we remember—or maybe even learn—who it is we really are . . . where the things that really matter are reinforced, and the values we cherish are etched into our hearts so we don't forget them. As my southern friend Jim Lowry's Pappy said to him every time Jim went out on a date, "Son, remember who you are." Can you remember whose name you bear, whose house you belong to? Can you remember who you really are?

One of our most cherished traditions in our church is the service of renewal of our baptismal vows. At the beginning of the year, we celebrate our true identity in the household of Jesus Christ: "Child of the covenant, you are sealed by the Holy Spirit, and marked as Christ's own forever." Like growing up in a family, the meaning of our identity doesn't become clear all at once but takes hold over time.

In fact, the apostle Paul suggests that being a Christian is less like being born into a family and more like an adoption. I'm reminded of our friends the Spencers, who adopted two little girls from China: Amy at twenty months old, and two years later, Suzy at three-and-a-half years old. (The girls are only six months apart, but they tell everyone they are *not* twins.) When Suzy was adopted, Amy wasted no time in showing her the ropes in her new family. Suzy didn't join her family with a full-formed understanding of what it meant to be a Spencer, but she learned. And she learned from her adopted sister. That's how it is for us in the household of God: we don't start with a full understanding of what it means to bear the name of Christ, but we learn. And we learn in large part from one another, from our sisters and brothers in Christ who welcome us in and show us the ropes.

For some of us, it's harder than for others, and our formation as children of God requires gentleness, forbearance, and endless patience. A few years ago I visited a psychiatric hospital directed by one of our church members. Bruce wanted to show me around, in part because it was his faith that prompted him to serve the mentally ill—not exactly a lucrative field for hospital administrators. As Bruce walked me through the various units—chemical dependency, chronic mental illness, self-inflicted injuries (largely teenage girls), eating disorders (ditto), he paused to greet each patient by name and ask how he or she was.

What got to me most was the long-term foster-care unit, where thirty children live for an average of two years. They are wards of the state, a drop in the bucket of the more than two thousand children the Department of Children and Family Services has in residential care. As Bruce walked me down the hall, he'd quietly say, "This child has the perfect imprint of an iron on his back," or "This girl was abused since she was a toddler." One young teenage girl we greeted was on the floor picking up shredded pieces of paper. She said she'd gotten mad and ripped up everything, and now she had to clean it up. Bruce bent over and whispered something encouraging to her, and as we left he said to me, "These children have to learn from scratch what it means to be children, how to interact, how to treat each other with decency and respect, how to be loved—what it means to be children of God."

Dear friends, a huge part of being the church is learning what it means to be children of God, what it means to come home to God's house. We are learning how to treat each other with respect and decency. We are learning, gradually, the language, the culture, the household rules. We are learning the intimate privilege of calling God *Abba*, Daddy. We are learning the family story:

> How God has many children, but loves each one of us
> How God keeps looking after us, even when we've behaved badly
> How God sets appropriate limits for us and consequences when we blow it
> How God has wonderful hopes for us, and desires our help in the family business, the business of the wholeness and healing of the world.

We are not learning all this on our own: Christ himself came to us, to show us the way; and indeed, we've been blessed with these brothers and sisters in Christ all around us, to help us, to show us the ropes, to help us be part of the family.

And when we forget who we are, or when we get lost and cannot find our way home, or when we are so broken that we cannot get back on our own, our family does what we cannot do on our own: they bring us back home . . . even if it means taking off the very roof to bring us in. This is the power of the Christian community. I love today's Gospel reading, the story of the paralytic:

Some people came, bringing to him a paralyzed man, carried by four of them. And when they could not bring him to Jesus because of the crowd, they removed the roof above him; and after having dug through it, they lay down the mat on which the paralytic lay. When Jesus saw *their* faith, he said to the paralytic, "Son, your sins are forgiven. . . . stand up, take your mat and go to your home."

Chances are you've been on one side or the other of this equation, and maybe you've been on both: the one who is carried in to Jesus' home or the one who does the carrying. So much of what we do in our churches is like that: coaching kids at Boys and Girls Clubs, building Habitat homes, filling food-pantry shelves, or feeding the homeless. But it's also what we do for one another, the tender mercies we provide in our own family of faith, in this affluent community that strives so hard to be strong and resilient and self-reliant and not in need of anything, thank you. Yet we know better, don't we? Chances are you've been both giver and receiver in this dear household of God. There is so much giving and receiving here:

> Stephen Ministers who tend to the grieving, the sick, the lonely, the sad . . . and those who are carried by them when they cannot stand on their own
> The knitters of the Prayer-Shawl ministry . . . and the ones whose shoulders are wrapped in their mantles of love
> The deacons who bring food and give rides during illnesses and bereavement . . . and all who need their service
> The prayer chain who lift people up to the Everlasting Arms . . . and the ones who cannot lift themselves
> The men's and women's Bible studies who write notes of comfort and encouragement . . . and all of us who are blessed by these kind and necessary ministrations

As for me, I will never forget the kindness shown me many years ago in Portland, when we lost our baby far into our pregnancy: the flowers and the notes and the simple gift of chicken soup and homemade bread . . . all this was love that carried me when I was utterly broken by sorrow, and all of this carried me home.

We are hungry, all of us. And often we are lost. But God provides for us a place of healing, a place of belonging, a family of faith in which we discover who we really are, a shelter that welcomes us to find our way home. It is easy, I suppose, to take this home, God's house, for granted. It is easy to find ourselves grazing on the programs of the church, to forget why we're here, to lose ourselves in committees and board meetings. It is easy to get distracted from building "beloved community," where everyone who walks into our doors can feel the "shelter, nurture and spiritual fellowship of the children of God." But if we forget, or doubt that it matters, all we have to do is look around to the lives that God has touched through the love of regular Christians, imperfect Christians like you and me, who call God's house our home.

It wasn't the programs or the committees or any other activity that prompted Ann Lamott to bring her young son, Sam, to church. She asks,

> You might wonder why I make this strapping, exuberant boy come with me most weeks, and if you were to ask, this is what I would say. "I make him because I can. I outweigh him by nearly seventy-five pounds." But that is only part of it. The main reason is that I want to give him what I found in the world, which is to say, a path and a little light to see by. Most of the people I know who have what I want—which is to say, purpose, heart, balance, gratitude, joy—are people with a deep sense of spirituality. They are people in community, who practice their faith. . . . They follow a brighter light than the glimmer of their own candle; they are part of something beautiful. . . . Our funky little church is filled with people who are working for peace and freedom, who are out there on the streets and inside praying, and they are home writing letters, and they are at the shelters with giant platters of food.
>
> When I was at the end of my rope, the people at St. Andrew tied a knot in it for me and helped me hold on. The church became my home in the old meaning of *home*—that is where, when you show up, they have to let you in. They let me in. They even said, "You come back now." [And] no matter how bad I am feeling, how lost or lonely or frightened, when I see the faces of the people at my church, and hear their tawny voices, I can always find my way home.

"O Lord, our hearts are restless till they find their rest in thee," Augustine said. O Lord, our hearts are restless . . . until they find their way home.

ACKNOWLEDGMENTS

Marjorie Thompson, *Soul Feast* (Louisville, KY: Westminster John Knox Press, 1995).
Joseph Small, *The Great Ends of the Church* (Louisville, KY: Witherspoon Press, 2003).
Nick Barger, *A New and Right Spirit: Creating an Authentic Church in a Consumer Culture* (Herndon, VA: Alban Institute, 2005).
Ann Lamott, *Traveling Mercies* (NY: Pantheon, 1999).

6

Treasure Seekers

Jennifer Oraker Holz

"Do not store up for yourselves treasures on earth, where moth and rust destroy, and where thieves break in and steal. But store up for yourselves treasures in heaven, where moth and rust does not destroy, and where thieves do not break in and steal. For where your treasure is, there your heart will be also.

"The eye is the lamp of the body. If your eyes are healthy, your whole body will be full of light. But if your eyes are unhealthy, your whole body will be full of darkness. If then the light within you is darkness, how great is the darkness!

"No one can serve two masters. Either you will hate the one and love the other, or you will be devoted to the one and despise the other. You cannot serve both God and money.

Matt. 6:19–24 TNIV

*I*n May of 1992 I graduated from college and found out that the internship I was planning on for the coming year was no longer an option. So, a week before graduation I was jobless, penniless, and uncertain what my next step would be. I had a fair amount of student loans. What was I going to do? I spent the next several weeks living with friends and pondering my future. It ended up being a very rich season. I experienced that window of time between finishing school and not yet having to respond to the real world. I wasn't paying bills; I wasn't meeting deadlines; and I could take time to listen to God about my future.

For many of us, the month of May represents a month of celebration, a time of endings and new beginnings. For somewhere between fifteen and twenty-five years of our lives, we finish one grade, take a short break, and get ready to move up to the adventure of the next grade. Eventually we graduate and get ready to enter the real world with a real job and a real paycheck. You may have been out of school for some time, but I think the rhythm of the school calendar stays with us. It is hard-wired into our souls. Given that, the month of May is a time when our hearts are ready for a breath of fresh air. We are ready for a summer break, anticipating new things and hopeful that a new season is about to begin in our lives.

We aren't sure exactly when Jesus preached his Sermon on the Mount, but it has always seemed likely to me that it must have been in the springtime. Jesus points to the birds of the air and the lilies of the field while he speaks—springtime illustrations of God's love and care for us. Spring is a good time to talk about life change, about the in-breaking of the kingdom of God, about where our hearts are and where God might be calling us to initiate heart changes.

Perhaps, then, it's a good time for us to hear something from the Sermon on the Mount. Jesus has a few things to say to us about money, about wealth, about what we treasure. And given the difficult economic times we are living through right now, we need to hear a word from God.

The Context

The Sermon on the Mount is found in Matthew, chapters 5, 6, and 7. Jesus' traveling ministry of proclamation and healing has led to the gathering of crowds from all over Israel. In his first main teaching in Matthew's Gospel, Jesus sets forth moral and ethical considerations in God's kingdom. Here we learn that an authentic relationship with him and with the Father is shaped by obedience to his commands. Let's look briefly at the overarching themes Jesus addresses in the three chapters of this extended sermon.

Chapter 5 is what Dale Bruner calls the "mercy" chapter. It is all about how we treat others and how we relate to others. In chapter 6, we find the "faith" chapter. This chapter unpacks how we are created to relate to God. And in chapter 7, we find the warnings of Jesus, or what Bruner calls the "justice" chapter. Here we discover what happens within us when we don't put into practice Jesus' instruction.

In the Sermon on the Mount, Jesus makes radical demands on his listeners. Yet "in his commands," Bruner says, "Jesus is alive. For in believing response to Jesus' commands, people come to life." The teachings of the Sermon on the Mount are not just words to ponder and study; they are the Word of God—words that are alive and empowered by the Spirit of God. The wise one puts his words into practice. Jesus' call is to listen and respond!

Our passage comes from chapter 6, the "faith" chapter, which opens with these words by Jesus: "Beware of practicing your piety before others in order to be seen by them." Jesus specifically mentions three acts of piety, three ways of living faithfully: giving, praying, and fasting. Jesus says that we are not to be hypocrites who give alms in order to be praised, who pray in order to be seen, who fast in order to show others our self-denial. Jesus recognizes the reality that many of us are motivated by the prospect of being noticed and admired by others. How we all long to be liked and to be seen by others as worthy and valuable! It feels good to be observed while doing good deeds or helping out a person in need. Many of us are eager for the praise and affirmation of others.

But while chapter 6 begins by warning us against the incentive of being noticed by others, it ends by calling us to care most deeply about how God sees us: "But strive first for the kingdom of God and his righteousness," Jesus says. The chapter narrates a progression of change, of transformation, of conversion (if you will) from having hearts that are motivated by the approval of others to hearts that beat in a genuine desire to seek God's approval and to strive for his kingdom. And right in the middle of this progression is where we find our Scripture for today. Hear it again:

> Do not store up for yourselves treasures on earth, where moth and rust consume and where thieves break in and steal; but store up for yourselves treasures in heaven, where neither moth nor rust consumes and where thieves do not break in and steal. For where your treasure is, there your heart will be also.

Treasure and Our Hearts

Jesus' words are about our hearts, about what we treasure, and the connection between the two. When we think about the *heart* today, we typically think about the place of emotion, intense feeling, even love or romance. If I say I am *heartsick* or have a *heartache*, I most likely mean I have experienced a breakup with a romantic partner or a rift with a close friend.

When we hear Tony Bennett singing, "I left my heart in San Francisco," we hear from a man who yearns for his home, a man who loves being in the city by the bay. On the other hand (and for those of us from another generation) when we hear Jon Bon Jovi singing, "Shot through the heart / And you're to blame," we know he is talking about a girl who led him on, played games with his heart, and left him. In contrast, to be softhearted means to be sensitive, open, and teachable. We like being around softhearted people. On the other end of the spectrum, hardhearted people are often stubborn, resistant, and not easy to be around.

When we see a heart as a symbol, then, it usually means love or strong feeling. "I 'heart' you" means "I love you." A bumper sticker that reads, "I 'heart' golden retrievers" or "I 'heart' pit bulls" means those dogs make that person's heart flutter. Of course, if we see a heart symbol on a menu, it means something is low in fat and good for your heart. As a culture we have recently become much more aware and worried about heart disease, so the phrases "heart healthy" or "heart smart" mean that something is physically good for the heart as an organ.

But, mostly, we associate the heart with feeling, emotion, and love.

In the biblical understanding, the term *heart* means something different from how we use the word today. Yes, it does include emotion and feeling, but it also encompasses much more. In the New Testament, your heart is your center; it is the center of spiritual life and the place within you where God shows himself to you. The heart represents your inner life and is the seat of the soul, spirit, will, and intellect. To *love God with all your heart* is not just to feel strongly about God but to love him with all your mind and soul and strength; it is to love him with every choice, every action, every thought, and every muscle of your being.

So, when Jesus says, "Where your treasure is, there will your heart be also," He's making a huge statement. *Whatever* it is that you love, value, cherish, adore, store up—that is what drives your life. Those are the things that will ultimately shape who you are as a person. Jesus' words in this passage don't just concern being careful about what you put in your storage unit, or your garage, or your basement. Rather, these words have everything to do with what ultimately makes you into the person you are.

The original Greek reads this way: *Don't treasure treasure on earth*. The same word is used as a verb and then as a noun. It does mean to "store up"— but it's more the act of cherishing that leads to storing it up. In other words, don't value the wrong things; don't fill up your heart or your mind with the things that don't last, that don't matter; the things that can be destroyed, stolen, or disappear at any moment. Jesus bids his followers never to regard earthly possessions as treasure.

Having said that, let's start with our storage units, our garages and our basements, because that is where we find things that moth and rust destroy and where thieves break in and steal.

Treasure on Earth

What treasures do you store up here on earth? Each of us could probably write down a fairly healthy list. What things have you stored up? And why you have saved them?

We have been raised in a culture that encourages us to stockpile material possessions. We treasure our "stuff," and we are very good at accumulating it. The American Dream is all about having enough "stuff." We save and strive and work so we can have, possess, keep.

We put our house on the market last summer, and in that process got a storage unit so we could move stuff out of our house to give it a more "roomy" feel. We were amazed at how much "junk" we have accumulated. Even after moving out a lot of our possessions, our house still felt full of stuff.

We live in a culture of accumulation . . . where we learn to value stuff. It's about comfort and security and peace of mind—and maybe at some point, when we have enough, we are supposed to feel all those things. But what is enough? "Just a little more than I have now" is what our culture generally says. The problem is that it is the very nature of treasure on earth never to have quite enough and always to be striving for a little more, to go for the next level. It is the nature of *having* that breeds discontentment within us. Into all of this, Jesus says, "Don't store up treasure on earth."

Have you ever talked to someone who has been through a fire, or a tornado, or a flood and lost everything they owned? It's usually a clarifying time. While they may wince at losing their possessions, as long as their families and friends are safe, they discover their true treasures are the people they love.

Lately, many of us are taking inventory of our losses in the stock market or the shrinking of the retirement funds we have been counting on. There is ample opportunity to reflect on our disappointments and the shattered dreams that we built around those funds. It is painful.

Pastor and theologian Dale Bruner pushes us to think a little more deeply about these words of Jesus. He writes that it is not just our money or material possessions that constitute treasure on earth; it is also our passions, the things we esteem, whatever it is we desire and pursue here on earth. As human beings, we are treasure seekers, searching for valuable items, both tangible or intangible.

Jesus is getting at the reality that when our hearts are focused on earthly treasure, they become drastically constricted. When our treasure becomes what we have or what we possess, our hearts shrink and become stagnant. Everything that we could possibly accumulate on earth is merely a finite quantity. And, as the old cliché goes, we can't take any of it with us. Read through Ecclesiastes for a dose of this reality. From an eternal perspective, treasuring earthly possessions is a vain pursuit, a mere chasing after vapor.

Treasure in Heaven

So, if it is true (as Bruner says) that to be human is to be a treasure seeker, then what is it that we are supposed to be chasing after? Jesus does more than repudiate our desire to seek after things of passing value and to store them up. Going far beyond that, he changes our focus, telling us what is truly valuable. He gives us a treasure map leading us to riches that will truly satisfy, treasure that won't disintegrate with time or corrode in bad weather.

"Store up treasure in heaven," Jesus says. Throughout chapter 5, Jesus' words build toward this command: *Listen*! Don't show off your acts of faith for *others* to see, but do your acts of faithful piety *in secret* for the approval of your *heavenly Father*. Give to the needy quietly; pray in your closet and close the door; forego food with a smile on your face. Jesus Christ points to the treasure of a heart that is focused on our heavenly Father. Store up *that* treasure, he says—the treasure of the Father's approval, the words "Well done, my good and faithful servant" that can come only from God.

But how does this change happen? It's one thing to say that we should simply change our focus from earth to heaven. It's quite another thing to do it. Our hearts are bombarded every day with the message of materialism, with the lure of wealth and possessions. The chasm from verse 19 to verse 20 is enormous. I can't change my own heart. Oh—maybe for a day or two I can make some changes, but real heart change? I'm not sure that's within my power.

It is God's work to change us. It is God's work to transform our hearts. Our work is to *hear* the Word and *respond* in faith. Heart changes happen slowly, over time, as we submit ourselves to the Word of God and choose to act on what we hear. Heart change happens as we act in obedience to God's word. And as we live out God's instruction, we begin to treasure the right things.

C. S. Lewis said the following in *Mere Christianity* about the process of heart change: "Every time you make a choice you are turning the central part of you [the heart], the part of you that chooses, into something a little different from what it was before. And taking your life as a whole, with all your innumerable choices, all your life long you are slowly turning this central thing either into a heavenly creature or into a hellish creature."

When our hearts are focused on God and the things of heaven, our hearts become open to limitless possibilities, expanding to encompass eternity. The writer of Ecclesiastes, who called earthly pursuits "vanity," also wrote that God has set our hearts at eternity; we were made for bigger things than this earth has to offer!

In the twelfth chapter of Romans, Paul writes, "Do not be conformed to this world, but be transformed by the renewing of your minds." Day by day we are being reshaped by the Spirit of God as we choose to engage with the Father's mind, heart, and Word in the midst of the community of other believers striving to do the same. In this way, we begin to move together from seeking earthly treasure to striving first for the kingdom of God.

Seek the Treasure of the Father's Heart

This is a strange message to be preaching on Mother's Day. The emphasis of Jesus' words seem to be "seek the treasure of the Father's heart," which sounds like a good Father's day sermon. However, it is an appropriate sermon to preach on Mother's Day or Father's Day, or *any* day that we celebrate our love for another person, for it is the love of God the Father that orders our love for others.

Without the priority of seeking the Father's love and the Father's heart first, our love for others is not the best it can be. Without the priority of the Father's love, our hearts get sidetracked into treasuring what others can give us rather than treasuring the person that God has given to us. Without the priority of the Father's love, our hearts move in pursuit of earthly things—money, possessions, status, wealth, approval from others, and the list goes on.

Seeking relationship with God our Father is a quiet, gentle, relational pursuit that is done in the secret places of our hearts, and done today without worrying about tomorrow. It's a day-by-day, moment-by-moment, heart-shaping movement towards a God who has created us, loves us, knows us, and longs to breathe life into us.

As we pause to remember and honor our mothers today, it also seems like a good time to stop and think about what we treasure in this life. Jesus encourages us to treasure God, for in treasuring God we learn to treasure one another. Seek the treasure of the Father's heart, for where your treasure is . . . there too will you find your heart.

Amen.

ACKNOWLEDGMENTS:

Dale Bruner, *Matthew: A Commentary. Vol. 1, The Christbook* (Grand Rapids: Eerdmans, 1987).

Geoffrey Bromiley & Gerhard Kittell, eds. *Theological Dictionary of the New Testament*, vol. III.

John Nolland, *The Gospel of Matthew* (NIGTC).

R. V. G. Tasher, *The Gospel According to St. Matthew* (Tyndale NT Commentaries).

7

The Ministry of Reconciliation as Spiritual Fellowship

Jin S. Kim

> *For the love of Christ urges us on, because we are convinced that one has died for all; therefore all have died. And he died for all, so that those who live might live no longer for themselves, but for him who died and was raised for them.*
>
> *From now on, therefore, we regard no one from a human point of view; even though we once knew Christ from a human point of view, we know him no longer in that way. So if anyone is in Christ, there is a new creation: everything old has passed away; see, everything has become new! All this is from God, who reconciled us to himself through Christ, and has given us the ministry of reconciliation; that is, in Christ God was reconciling the world to himself, not counting their trespasses against them, and entrusting the message of reconciliation to us. So we are ambassadors for Christ, since God is making his appeal through us; we entreat you on behalf of Christ, be reconciled to God.*
>
> 2 Cor. 5:14–20

*I*n January of 2004 a group of mostly second-generation members of a Korean immigrant congregation in Minneapolis was blessed by our "mother church" to launch a multicultural community called Church of All Nations. We were chartered with great expectations by our presbytery and denominational leaders, but no one knew if one hundred mostly young Korean Americans could actually become a Church of All Nations; many thought the name was a bit premature, if not presumptuous.

Today, we are a healthy, midsized congregation that is roughly 30 percent Asian, 37 percent white, 22 percent black, and 10 percent Latino, with more than twenty-five nations represented in our membership. Our pastoral staff includes people from Korea, Kenya, Sudan, Brazil, China, Japan, Cote d'Ivoire, and the United States (both Euro- and African American). Our session and board of deacons also fully reflect this diversity.

We are one of a handful of congregations in the United States with no ethnic majority and sizable groups of the four major racial categories of white, black, Asian, and Latino. But we actually have even more denominational background diversity than ethnic diversity, drawing as many Catholics, Episcopalians, and Lutherans as we do Pentecostals, Baptists, and Evangelical Free. Our highly visible commitment to ecumenical unity may be one reason that out of the twenty-five new members we recently welcomed, the vast majority had no Presbyterian background. We also draw equal numbers of Republicans and Democrats, and we address politics, racism, the economy, war, and peace head on.

Our central mission is to live into the ministry of reconciliation, and it is happening in all kinds of wonderful ways here. For instance, in January of 2006 we moved from our Korean mother church into the building of a declining white PC(USA) congregation, Shiloh Bethany Church, which had plenty of room. We rented space for a few months, but then Shiloh Bethany asked if they might merge with us. At the end of July the congregation that was founded in 1884 was dissolved, and all of its members became members of Church of All Nations.

Incidentally, 1884 is the year that PC(USA) missionaries first arrived on the shores of my home country of Korea. So we came full circle, historically speaking. One of the key reasons for the union of Shiloh Bethany with the Church of All Nations was the growing recognition of the need to be a new kind of church for an increasingly multicultural population in Columbia Heights and the entire Twin Cities area. Church of All Nations fit that need very well. After more than three years together, all of the original Shiloh Bethany members remain members to this day—praise God!

We witness many signs of growth in our midst, but the most important thing is that people are filled with joy, hope, and genuine love for one another across all kinds of lines, dismantling barriers erected by church and society, history and culture. For decades, Shiloh Bethany members had prayed that their sanctuary would be full again and that the building would be restored to its original condition. Who knew that God would answer the prayers of this typical, small, white church through a young, multicultural church? Who knew that a new church would own a beautiful, sizable building overlooking a gorgeous lake and be debt free within three years of its existence? Who knew that by committing to the ministry of reconciliation, two congregations would form a new spiritual fellowship that would shelter and nurture so many of God's children from around the world?

Many of us who began this journey assumed that we would be dealing with much more conflict as many cultures and worldviews added to the complexity of congregational dynamics. What we have discovered, to our delight, is the exact opposite. The very decision to join a church in which one chooses to be a minority seems to draw the kind of people who are willing to "lay down their sword" of power and privilege. The Korean American founders had to set the example first. Today, all of us seem to be caught up in a virtuous cycle of lifting up and valuing other individuals and cultures, "considering others better than oneself." The culture of public confession, corporate repentance, joyful celebration, and vulnerable relationality that we have cultivated here is key to understanding the dynamism and eschatological hope evident in our life together.

We live in the time between the "already" and "not yet." Our church sees itself between Pentecost in Acts 2 and the coming kingdom in Revelation 7, when all nations, tribes, and tongues will glorify God together in one voice. We feel called to be an ecumenical church that embodies the major spiritual roots of the early church—to be simultaneously rational, sacramental, and pentecostal. We are also convinced that only intentional movement away from rigid denominationalism toward visible unity will lead the global church to recover its identity as "one holy catholic and apostolic" church. We are a high-risk, low-anxiety church where anything is possible, including the possibility of failure. The only poverty we fear is the poverty of imagination. We feel blessed with God's abundance and grace.

I want to describe now something of the theology and practice of our congregation, giving particular attention to the way our diverse community engages in the ministry of reconciliation. In this way we become a place where *all* children of God find "shelter, nurture, and spiritual fellowship."

Reconciliation as a Central Theme

The Church of All Nations intentionally transitioned from an ethnocentric ministry to a multicultural church not for the sake of aesthetic diversity but for the compelling call of racial and cultural reconciliation. Reconciliation is more a mystery to embrace than a technique to perfect. It is a word both mundane and otherworldly. We reconcile our checkbooks, but can we really be reconciled to God and to one another this side of heaven?

Dietrich Bonhoeffer in his *Letters and Papers from Prison* captures the mysterious nature of reconciliation in this passage:

> Reconciliation and redemption, regeneration and the Holy Spirit, love of our enemies, cross and resurrection, life in Christ and Christian disciple-

ship—all these things are so difficult and so remote that we hardly venture any more to speak of them. In the traditional words and acts we suspect that there may be something quite new and revolutionary, though we cannot as yet grasp or express it.

The ancient practices of confession, repentance, forgiveness, and reconciliation have become remote in the modern church. Obviously, the church has not been untouched by the materialism, hedonism, and nihilistic spiral of radical individualism in the West. The pragmatic arrangement between church and state in Europe and North America has also conspired to weaken the church's prophetic witness. Bonhoeffer continues, "Our church, which has been fighting in these years only for its self-preservation, as though that were an end in itself, is incapable of taking the word of reconciliation and redemption to mankind and the world."

How does the church speak with authority on a subject as radical as reconciliation if it has been domesticated by the surrounding culture and the political establishment? South African theologian John de Gruchy puts it this way: "The problem was that the Church in Germany, and by inference elsewhere, had become captive to bourgeois culture, and thus its use of biblical concepts confirmed rather than challenged the status quo." Karl Barth felt compelled to write the Barmen Declaration because the German church had neither the theology nor the courage to counter the radical nationalism of Hitler's regime. It is a chilling reminder that the co-optation of the church and its holy Scriptures can lead to devastating results.

De Gruchy also helps the modern church to understand that the word reconciliation became current in Christian discourse through the Latin *reconciliatio*, a Vulgate translation of the Greek *katallagê*. In the New Testament, Paul used this word as an allusion to God's saving work in Jesus Christ. It is an important word that encapsulates God's cosmic enterprise of eschatological salvation. De Gruchy notes that the Anglican theologian Rowan Williams refers to reconciliation as "a seductively comfortable word, fatally close to 'consensus.'"

Reconciliation is much closer in meaning to redemption (God's saving work) than to consensus. In that light, reconciliation is at the core of the biblical narrative and the gospel embodied in Jesus Christ. Karl Barth made reconciliation the central theme of his *Church Dogmatics*. Concerning reconciliation, he wrote, "We enter that sphere of Christian knowledge in which we have to do with the heart of the message received by and laid upon the Christian community, and therefore with the heart of the Church's dogmatics." And in *Evangelical Theology*, a theological swan song of lectures delivered in the United States a few years before his death, Barth declared, "The new event is the world's reconciliation with God, which was announced in the Old Testament and fulfilled in the New Testament by Jesus Christ."

A relatively recent statement of faith incorporated into the Presbyterian Church (U.S.A.)'s *Book of Confessions* was ratified and adopted in 1967. The introduction to this confession states, "Modestly titled, the Confession of 1967 is built around a single passage of Scripture: In Christ God was reconciling the world to himself." The Presbyterian Church confessed in that turbulent time of American history that reconciliation is a mandate for the church in all times: "God's reconciling work in Jesus Christ and the mission of reconciliation to which he has called his church are the heart of the gospel in any age. Our generation stands in peculiar need of reconciliation in Christ. Accordingly, this Confession of 1967 is built upon that theme."

The Confession of 1967 goes on to claim that *since* "God was reconciling the world to himself," *therefore* the church calls men and women to be reconciled to one another. The Church of All Nations has a strong sense of missional calling, a sense that we have been called out from the world to minister to the world. We are not to focus on security or self-preservation but are called to risk our money, time, and talents, indeed our very life for the sake of sharing the good news in Jesus Christ with the world. The Confession of 1967 articulates this concept most clearly in the section titled "The Mission of the Church":

> To be reconciled to God is to be sent into the world as his reconciling community. This community, the church universal, is entrusted with God's message of reconciliation and shares his labor of healing the enmities which separate men from God and from each other. Christ has called the church to this mission and given it the gift of the Holy Spirit.

The Belhar Confession of 1982–1986, produced by churches suffering from apartheid in South Africa, also makes reconciliation its central theme. Previously, the Dutch Reformed Church had segregated itself from all nonwhite Dutch Reformed Christians, who then were subdivided further into Coloured, Black, and Indian Dutch Reformed denominations. The Belhar Confession states clearly,

> We believe that Christ's work of reconciliation is made manifest in the Church as the community of believers who have been reconciled with God and with one another; . . . that this unity can be established only in freedom and not under constraint; that the variety of spiritual gifts, opportunities, backgrounds, convictions, as well as the various languages and cultures, are by virtue of the reconciliation in Christ, opportunities for mutual service and enrichment within the one visible people of God.

In experiencing the joy and wonder of becoming a reconciled community, the members of the Church of All Nations seem to have a growing passion to share that message widely—in the local community, in the larger church, across denominational lines, and across national borders. The mission of our congregation is wholly in agreement with the Confession of 1967 and the Belhar Confession—that the ministry of reconciliation must be at the very heart of our existence as a Christian community.

Trading Places and Creating Spaces

Although the Greek word for "reconciliation" or "reconcile" appears only fifteen times in the New Testament, and mostly in the Pauline letters, it serves an important purpose in helping to unravel God's ultimate plan of salvation. According to John de Gruchy, "All of them are compounds of the Greek *allassō*, "to exchange," and this in turn is derived from *allos* meaning "the other." So reconciliation carries with it the sense of exchanging places with "the other" and therefore of being in solidarity with, rather than against, "the other." Put simply, reconciliation begins by asking the simple question, What would it be like to walk in the other's shoes?

Reconciliation is to *exchange* with the other, and the beginning of exchange is the act of hospitality. My hunch is that people show hospitality to another because they can imagine what it would be like to be in the other's place. Hospitality is motivated by imaginatively trading places with a stranger or a guest. Hospitality is a central feature of what it means to be a genuine Christian community modeled after the life and teachings of Jesus. Even the sacraments of baptism and the Lord's Supper can be understood as an extension of God's hospitality and friendship to God's creation.

Henry Nouwen says, "Hospitality . . . means primarily the creation of a free space where the stranger can enter and become a friend instead of an enemy." Trading places, even evocatively, will move us to have compassion in "creating space" and granting freedom for the stranger in a way that we would wish for ourselves. This space is not to be confused with isolation and loneliness. Nouwen goes on to say,

> The paradox of hospitality is that it wants to create emptiness where strangers can enter and discover themselves as created free; free to sing their own songs, speak their own languages, dance their own dances; free also to leave and follow their own vocations. Hospitality is not a subtle invitation to adopt the lifestyle of the host, but the gift of a chance for the guest to find his own.

Hospitality is the fertile soil on which reconciliation can flower. In our congregation, hospitality is preached, practiced, and embodied first and foremost in the Sunday worship service. Our practice of worship is specifically crafted to create and sustain spiritual fellowship.

In our proclamation of the gospel we use the gift of imagination to trade places with the oppressed in the Bible, in history, in the world, and in our midst. In our proclamation we create space for the marginalized by naming the injustices, fears, and hardships that they confront every day. If our congregational culture was such that it was not "polite" to speak openly of racism, sexism, personal prejudice, and structural sin, there would be no "space" for those seeking hospitality to be themselves with their histories. Instead, they would be expected to accommodate the prevailing culture, to "adopt the lifestyle of the host." This would lead not to reconciliation but to sterilization. At the Church of All Nations, we believe that the Christian community must proclaim reconciliation everywhere—from the rooftops as well as from the pulpit—as God's good news for humanity.

Our worship service also regularly includes testimony, a practice we borrow from the great African American church tradition. In line with the Reformation principle of the "priesthood of all believers," we find that it liberates all God's children to minister to one another. To make space for testimony, the preacher "trades places" with a congregation member. When a testimony requires a significant portion of time, the sermon is replaced entirely by the congregational testimony, but more typically our members give a brief testimony during the offertory as an offering to the Lord. At least twice a year, the entire service will be devoted to congregational testimonies from the floor as members rise up spontaneously to speak of God's presence and activity in their lives.

Almost always, these have been profound moments of an outpouring of compassion, tears, laughter, understanding, and transformation, resulting in the deepening of spiritual fellowship. Many of our members have taken great risks to reveal their brokenness and shame before the entire church, wondering if this act of vulnerability would become one more wound. Happily, this has not been the case. If people had judged others for being poor, black, white, barren, pregnant out of wedlock, alcoholic, depressed, or diseased, judgment was replaced quickly with hospitality and reconciliation through the power inherent in testimony, through the strength to be vulnerable. Jesus died naked on a cross. The fundamental message of our congregation in this regard has been, "Go and do likewise, and we, through Christ, will cover you with compassion, forgiveness and love."

We have also discovered that reconciliation can and must take sacramental form. In baptism God takes the initiative in reconciling the people to God's self. The Confession of 1967 states, "By humble submission to John's baptism, Christ joined himself to men in their need and entered upon his ministry of reconciliation in the power of the Spirit." In baptism, not only has Christ joined himself to humanity, but all the baptized are joined to one another in the fellowship of Christ's body. In our brokenness we are joined to Christ's broken body, a sign of God's reconciling and heartbreaking love for us.

The sacrament of the Lord's Supper is also an opportunity to experience divine reconciliation. The Confession of 1967 says, "The Lord's Supper is a celebration of the reconciliation of men with God and with one another, in which they joyfully eat and drink together at the table of their Savior." Sharing a common meal is one of the most ancient expressions of hospitality. This simple act has profound and even historical implications for the church's witness in the world. Consider the history of the church in South Africa. John de Gruchy relates that

> Holy Communion itself became the critical testing ground within the dominant Dutch Reformed Church in the mid nineteenth century when, because of the "weakness of some" white members, it became permissible to allow segregation at the sacrament. This eventually led to the segregation of the Dutch Reformed Church itself and provided theological support for what later became the policy of apartheid.

How different is the history of the church in America? Yet despite the persistent disobedience and rebellion of the church to carry out the ministry of reconciliation, God has not given up on the church. In the simple act of breaking bread and drinking the cup, God demonstrates God's commitment to reconciliation with humanity. *Since* we have been reconciled in our communion with God, *therefore*, in gratitude to God, we are compelled to be reconciled with our neighbors. God's initiative in reconciling with humanity makes possible reconciliation in sacramental community.

We have come to understand that the worship service is the locus of hospitality, spiritual fellowship, and reconciliation—a creative space for welcome, healing, and wholeness. The worship service can too often be reduced to individual penance, consumer-driven entertainment, a self-improvement seminar, or an institutional requirement. Nothing less than the liberation of the church's corporate imagination is required to transform the traditional service from mindless ritual to a space hospitable to the redemptive reconciliation of all God's children. In proclamation, testimony, and sacrament, the Church of All Nations strives to create such a sheltering and nurturing space.

Reconciliation as Ecclesial Practice

The local congregation is the primary locus of discipleship and Christian formation. In baptism, God welcomes us into his family through our incorporation into the body of Christ. In the Lord's Supper, we become a community that experiences *shalom*, a profound sense of peace and well-being, because our reconciliation with God in the Eucharist makes possible our reconciliation with one another. The church cannot be reduced to serving as a repository for individuals to be randomly reconciled privately with other individuals as a form of individual penance. Missiologist Inagrace Dietterich stresses that

> reconciliation—confession, judgment, and forgiveness—is not an individual and private matter, but an ecclesial practice that fosters, shapes, and sustains missional communities. . . .While central to the biblical understanding of the nature of salvation, reconciliation may be the most difficult practice for contemporary Christians even to consider, much less to actualize within their congregations.

Few would argue against the notion that reconciliation is a "most difficult practice," and yet we have been called to be the church engaged in the ministry of reconciliation. The church of Jesus Christ is nothing less than the "provisional demonstration" of "God reconciling the world to himself." The constitution of the Presbyterian Church (U.S.A.) is so bold as to claim, "The new reality revealed in Jesus Christ is the new humanity, a new creation, a new beginning for human life in the world: Sin is forgiven, reconciliation is accomplished, the dividing walls of hostility are torn down." What is shocking about this claim is the declarative way in which it is written: "Reconciliation *is* accomplished." Our experience tells us that no such thing has been accomplished in the church or in the world. However, in Christ, the *new reality* has been revealed and is even now unfolding. In Christ, and only in Christ, reconciliation *is* accomplished through the power of the cross. The church is called to live boldly into that new reality.

Reconciliation is a messy affair. Reconciliation is a costly affair. It is not a "technical rationality" but a "possible impossibility." The ministry of reconciliation is God's mandate to the church so that the church may be a gift to the world. The church is challenged not only to preach but to model reconciliation parabolically as a worshiping community that creates and sustains spiritual fellowship of all God's children. As God is both immanent and transcendent—*God with Us* and *God the Wholly Other*—so reconciliation is both inviting the other and releasing the other, mutual embrace and mutual release. In the reconciled fellowship of sheltering, nurturing, and sending, may God be worshiped and glorified by all the children of God.

Amen.

ACKNOWLEDGMENTS

Karl Barth, *Evangelical Theology* (Grand Rapids: Wm. B. Eerdmans Publishing Co., 1963).

David Bosch, *Transforming Mission* (New York: Orbis Books, 1991).

World Council of Churches, *Baptism, Eucharist and Ministry* (Geneva: World Council of Churches, 1982).

Inagrace Dietterich, "Missional Community" in *Missional Church,* Darrell L. Guder, ed. (Grand Rapids: William B. Eerdmans Publishing, 1998).

Presbyterian Church (U.S.A.), *The Constitution of the Presbyterian Church (U.S.A.),* Part I, *Book of Confessions* (Louisville, KY: Office of the General Assembly, 2007).

Presbyterian Church (U.S.A.), *The Constitution of the Presbyterian Church (U.S.A.),* Part II, *Book of Order* (Louisville, KY: Office of the General Assembly, 2007).

Presbyterian Church (U.S.A.), *A Study of the Belhar Confession* (Louisville, KY: Office of Theology and Worship, 2008).

8

Treasure in Our Hearts

Rodger Nishioka

Now every year [Jesus'] parents went to Jerusalem for the festival of the Passover. And when he was twelve years old, they went up as usual for the festival. When the festival was ended and they started to return, the boy Jesus stayed behind in Jerusalem, but his parents did not know it. Assuming that he was in the group of travelers, they went a day's journey. Then they started to look for him among their relatives and friends. When they did not find him, they returned to Jerusalem to search for him. After three days they found him in the temple, sitting among the teachers, listening to them and asking them questions. And all who heard him were amazed at his understanding and his answers. When his parents saw him they were astonished; and his mother said to him, "Child, why have you treated us like this? Look, your father and I have been searching for you in great anxiety." He said to them, "Why were you searching for me? Did you not know that I must be in my Father's house?" But they did not understand what he said to them. Then he went down with them and came to Nazareth, and was obedient to them. His mother treasured all these things in her heart.

And Jesus increased in wisdom and in years, and in divine and human favor.

Luke 2:41–52

We do not know much about Jesus' childhood. Certainly we have the two birth narratives in the Gospels of Matthew and Luke, but we have very little else between his dedication at the temple and his baptism by John when Jesus begins his public ministry . . . except for this one story related by Luke. Luke tells us that Jesus is twelve years old—on the verge of becoming a man according to Jewish tradition. It is one of the high holy days for the Hebrew people—the celebration of Passover. During high holy days, the great celebrations, all of the towns and villages throughout the countryside cleared out and people who were able journeyed to Jerusalem to be as close as possible to the temple. Pilgrims traveled from miles around. Passover is one of the greatest holy days for the Hebrew people, so Mary and Joseph and their young son, Jesus, went to Jerusalem. They traveled with other pilgrims, probably on foot since they were not wealthy and had no servants to carry them.

It was a two-day journey from Nazareth to Jerusalem. Mary and Joseph and the other pilgrims camped overnight in the Jordan River valley and then walked up the mountain to the plateau on which Jerusalem sits. They participated in the marvelous Passover celebration and then along with the other pilgrims began to head home to Nazareth. Mary and Joseph went a day's journey on the return trip and then, when they began to set up camp for the night, started to look for their son Jesus. Why didn't they realize that Jesus was not with them on the day's journey? I guess that Mary and Joseph assumed that their oldest was simply traveling with the larger group of family and friends. They were probably also distracted by having to care for their other children.

We know from later texts that Mary and Joseph went on to have other children. Jesus had younger brothers and sisters. Imagine growing up with Jesus Christ as an older brother. It puts a whole new dimension on the sibling rivalry concept! I can imagine one of Jesus' little brothers or sisters getting upset with Jesus and saying, "Oh, Jesus, you just think you're *so* perfect!" Jesus probably looked at them and smiled and shrugged. I imagine it wasn't very easy for those kids to win an argument with the Lord.

Anyway, Mary and Joseph are looking for Jesus, and you can imagine the conversation between the two parents. It's likely that it resembled conversations between parents today: Mary turns to her husband and asks, "Sweetheart, have you seen the Messiah?" Joseph looks blankly at his spouse and replies, "No, my matzo ball. Last time we talked, you said you were going to watch for the Lamb of God who taketh away the sins of the world."

Well, perhaps the conversation did not go exactly like that, but in a short time Mom and Dad realize that their son is not with them or their family or their friends. They race back to Jerusalem, a full day's journey, and search the city. Now, Jerusalem is a huge place. Three days of looking could be only the beginning. Eventually, nearing desperation, they overhear a conversation about this kid who has been in the temple for several days talking with the teachers and religious leaders and impressing them with his knowledge. They look at each other and realize in an instant that it is their son. They run to the temple, and they find him just sitting there, calmly talking. For five days, Jesus has been sitting with the scholars, listening to them, asking questions, and talking with them. Luke tells us that all who heard him, including the scholars, were amazed at his understanding and his responses.

Now, when Mary and Joseph find him they are "astonished." This is the English word scholars use to translate from the Bible's Greek. "Astonished" is not a bad translation, but when I read that, I think to myself, Mary and Joseph have lost their son now for at least five days, and when they find him they are "astonished"? I think there is more to it than that. Sure enough, if you look at the Greek you discover that the root of the word there is *ekplēsso*, which can be translated "amazed, astounded, or overwhelmed." Bible translators have elected to use the word "astonished," which is not a bad choice, but the Greek word can also have the sense of being "overwhelmed," sometimes with fright, sometimes with wonder, sometimes with joy, and sometimes with all three simultaneously. In our limited English, we get only the most common translation—"astonished." But a Greek hearer of this story would have understood that when Mary and Joseph found their son after searching for him they were amazed, astounded, and overwhelmed with fright, wonder, and joy.

So, overwhelmed with emotion, Mary asks her son a classic mother-type question: "Child, why have you treated us like this? Look, your father and I have been searching for you in great anxiety." And Jesus answers them with a question (which must have exasperated Mary even further): "Well, Mom and Dad, why were you searching for me? Didn't you know I must be in my Father's house?" Luke tells us that Mary and Joseph "did not understand what he said to them," which I think is Bible code language for "His parents did not calm down right away."

The rest of the passage tells us that they returned to Nazareth and Jesus was obedient to them—which is important. And then Luke tells us that in response to all this Mary "treasured all these things in her heart" and that Jesus grew in wisdom and in years, and in favor with God and people.

In response to being amazed, even overwhelmed, Mary *treasured all that had happened in her heart.* This wonderful story provides us with insight into what it means to live out the second great end of the church: "the shelter, nurture, and spiritual fellowship of the children of God." It seems to me that Mary reflects beautifully the essence of this sheltering and nurturing and spiritual fellowship. To shelter, nurture, and provide spiritual fellowship for the children of God is to *treasure.* And this treasuring is not a passive, Presbyterian, pew-potato kind of thing. It is active. I am sure that when Mary treasured all these things in her heart, Jesus knew it because he experienced it.

In our time and place, we treasure all the children of God when we truly see them, not as objects to be acted on but as ones who participate in ushering in the reign of God. We treasure all the children of God when we engage them in conversation, sharing our stories of faith with them and hearing their own stories of faith. We treasure the children of God every time we provide opportunities for spiritual growth and nurture through church school, and youth groups, and mission trips, and caring for families. We treasure the children of God when we pray for and with them.

There is an emerging body of research about youth that is at once frightening and thrilling. It focuses on a young person's "resilience." Simply put, their resilience seems to depend on whether or not youth can identify adults in their lives who treasure them just as Mary treasured Jesus. To measure a young person's resilience, researchers invited a random sample of young people to think of the worst possible thing they could imagine doing. Then they were asked to name adults in their life whom they could tell that they had done this worst possible thing and who would still love them. This resilience research seems to indicate that young people have to be able to name at least four adults who they believe treasure them. If they cannot name four—and here is the frightening part—then an alarming number of these young people will either be dead or in jail before they are twenty-one years-old.

I asked this question of young people in the church where I regularly worship here in Atlanta, and, thankfully, most could easily name more than four. But several struggled. One young person took two days, but she thought up four. I was surprised, though, when one young man named among his seven adults a woman in our congregation who I don't think is very pleasant. Later I pulled him aside and said, "You know, Ian, I was surprised that Mrs. Shelton is one of your adults. Are you friends?" "Friends? Are you kidding?" he replied incredulously. "Dude, she is a mean old lady!" I confessed that is exactly what I thought. But then Ian went on to explain that Mrs. Shelton taught his church school class when he was in third grade. She made them recite memory verses and always scolded them if they messed up. But Ian explained that while she was mean, even now she also always called him by name and stopped to talk with him whenever she saw him. She also sent him a birthday card every year. I didn't know any of this. Ian said that while she may seem a little mean, he thought she really loved him. (Plus, he still remembers those Bible verses.)

That is what treasuring is all about. It is what sheltering and nurturing and spiritual fellowship is all about. No doubt there are times when we are amazed, astounded, and even overwhelmed by our children, our youth . . . even our young adults, middle-aged adults, and older adults. And the mother of our Lord teaches us that the best response is to treasure each other in our hearts so that all children of God know that the One who created them in God's own image, redeemed them through God's only Son, and sustains them through God's Holy Spirit, treasures them in God's own heart forever.

May it be so. Amen.

3

The Maintenance
of Divine Worship

9

At This Table

Deborah Block

> On the first day of Unleavened Bread, when the Passover lamb is sacrificed, [Jesus'] disciples said to him, "Where do you want us to go and make the preparations for you to eat the Passover?" So he sent two of his disciples, saying to them, "Go into the city, and a man carrying a jar of water will meet you; follow him, and wherever he enters, say to the owner of the house, 'The Teacher asks, Where is my guest room where I may eat the Passover with my disciples?' He will show you a large room upstairs, furnished and ready. Make preparations for us there." So the disciples set out and went to the city, and found everything as he had told them; and they prepared the Passover meal.
>
> When it was evening, he came with the twelve. And when they had taken their places and were eating, Jesus said, "Truly I tell you, one of you will betray me, one who is eating with me." They began to be distressed and to say to him one after another, "Surely, not I?" He said to them, "It is one of the twelve, one who is dipping the bread into the bowl with me. For the Son of Man goes as it is written of him, but woe to that one by whom the Son of Man is betrayed! It would have been better for that one not to have been born.
>
> While they were eating, he took a loaf of bread, and after blessing it he broke it, gave it to them, and said, "This is my body." Then he took a cup, and after giving thanks he gave it to them, and all of them drank from it. He said to them, "This is my blood of the covenant, which is poured out for many. Truly I tell you, I will never again drink of the fruit of the vine until that day when I drink it new in the kingdom of God."
>
> Mark 14:12–25

This is the Lord's table"—standard language of the invitation to the Table—words worth digesting before we accept the invitation to "share the feast which he has prepared."

"This is the *Lord's* table." The house we are in is furnished simply and functionally. Pulpit and lectern, font and table, cross. One of the intriguing things about Mark's Gospel is the prominence of the house as a setting for Jesus' activity. Jesus has been in the house of Simon and Andrew, has had dinner in Levi's house, and after trips to neighboring towns has simply been "at home" in Capernaum, in his house, where he lived and ate and slept and received guests. He has been "at home" in his house, with chairs, and a bed, and a table.

"*This* is the Lord's table." It is a connection to Jesus in real time and place, doing something that people in every time and place do: gather, eat, commune. The table is basic furnishing and function. Life happens around tables. When we are old enough, we sit at the table. As children we eat at tables where we are corrected in our table manners, coached to say grace, told to eat with our mouth closed, taught to say, "Please" and "Thank you." As children we play at tables; we learn at tables. As adults we work at tables; we meet at tables; we communicate and negotiate and commit at tables. At tables we break bread and share it and pour out our hearts. We make deals and decisions, sign contracts, lift a glass to commiserate or celebrate our fortune, all at tables.

Faith happens around tables. When we are old enough, we come to this Table. As children of God, we eat at the Lord's Table with proper table manners, couched in the language of grace: eat with your heart open, say praise and thank you. God works at this Table. We meet God at this Table. We commit and commune. We accept God's gracious offer, seal the covenant, lift the cup to celebrate our faith. Jesus sat at table in the house of Simon the Leper, and faith happened there. An invitation extended and accepted; Jesus as guest and host. There was breaking and pouring, a good service for Jesus in a woman's anointing; good news for the world in proclaiming Jesus as Lord.

"This is the Lord's *table*"—a table, not an altar. Presbyterian worship space is distinctively marked by a "place for the reading of Scripture and the preaching of the Word, a font for Baptism, and a table suitable for the people's celebration of the Lord's Supper." This is a table, not an altar, because this is a meal and not a sacrifice. Another German Reformer named Martin—this one Bucer—was the one who substituted "Lord's Supper" for "Mass" and renamed the altar a "table." Four centuries later Roman Catholics followed suit when Vatican II required new churches to have a free-standing altar-table so that the priest could stand behind it, facing the people. At Immanuel Presbyterian Church we position the Table for visibility and access, setting it with symbols and service. The Table is at the center of our space. You pass the font to come and go, and when you are at the Table you stand under the cross. Whether we're serving the Lord's Supper or not, we set a chalice and a plate on the Table to remind us what it is and what it's for. We even add candles, just like a dining table in one's home.

And it is a *dining* table, because, after all, this is the Lord's *Supper.* And, in some places, it is literally so. The theological housecleaning of the Reformation included rearranging the worship furniture as well as renaming it. The altar was reborn a table, and the Table gave birth to the original church folding tables, set up across the front of the church or down the aisles so that the congregation could actually gather at table and sit, stand, or kneel to eat the bread and drink the wine family style! A community meal, communion of saints, yes; but Calvin spoke even more intimately, saying that at this Table God gathers us as God's own family, children, offspring.

The Reformation also brought an almost domestic simplicity to the Holy Table. Worship historian James White notes that the Swiss reformer Zwingli celebrated the Eucharist using the "common wooden platters and cups that each housewife must have scrubbed (we hope) daily." Zwingli was not fond of symbolism, but these simple wooden dishes expressed a clear message about the commonness of the common meal of the Lord's Supper.

"This is the Lord's Table." Bread and wine: one, the basic sustenance of every meal; the other, the festive substance of covenant joy. Bread and wine: gifts of life and salvation broken, poured out, shared. At any Jewish meal the host blesses the bread. At the Passover meal the host blesses the bread and the cup. At the Last Supper the host blessed the bread and the cup and the disciples. But the table fellowship would be broken by betrayal. The host would be broken by violence. But they would gather again, hungry for the bread of life, for forgiveness, for community, for table grace. They would gather at the Lord's Table and know him to be there.

Over the centuries good, faithful, reasonable Christians have argued where and how Jesus is present at his Table: In the *remembrance* of his life and death? In the *physical substances* of the bread and wine? Our Reformed tradition leans more to the consecration of the people rather than the consecration of the bread and wine (Bucer), but it is unapologetic about the mystery that happens at this table (Calvin). There is spiritual nourishment and the real presence of Christ at this table, a communion worked by the Holy Spirit. Jesus Christ is not *on* the table, in symbol or reality. "This is the *Lord's Table.*" Jesus Christ is present *at* this table. "He is always among his own people," as Calvin put it, "and breathes his life upon them, and lives in them, sustaining them, strengthening, quickening, keeping them unharmed, as if he were present in the body." At this table we are maintained in our worship and life. "Maintain"—keep in working order—sounds very Presbyterian! The root meaning and the heart of "maintain" are words meaning "hold in the hand." At this table we are held in God's hand, touched by grace. At this table Jesus Christ is immanent, Immanuel, God with us, in the flesh and blood of our own lives.

"This is the Lord's table."

When we gather here, accepting his invitation, we mind our table manners, our manner of life learned at this table. Remember? Eat with your heart open, say praise and thank you. Break the bread and share it. Feed one another as we have been fed. Make room for another person. Eat of the one loaf; drink of the one cup; commune as one community. Calvin taught us that the Lord intends the Supper to inspire us "to love, peace, and concord." Like a bread of many grains, was his analogy, so mixed together that one cannot be distinguished from another; "so it is fitting that in the same way we should be joined and bound together by such great agreement of minds that no sort of disagreement or division may intrude. And if you still might be thinking that all of this is a bit stale, chew on these words from Calvin as we come to the table in our time:

> None of the [brothers and sisters] can be injured, despised, rejected, abused, or in any way offended by us, without at the same time, injuring, despising, and abusing Christ by the wrongs we do. . . . We cannot disagree with our [brothers and sisters] without at the same time disagreeing with Christ. . . . We cannot love Christ without loving him in the [brothers and sisters]. . . . We ought to take the same care of our brothers' and sisters' bodies as we take care of our own; for they are members of our body. . . .

We are all touched by the pain of one; we are all touched by compassion when evil affects one. Hard to swallow? It is this essential ethical dimension of the Lord's Table that we set aside. Can we savor the mystery of the Table and ignore the misery of the world? Injury, rejection, abuse; love, peace, concord. What happens at this Table?

"None of the [brothers and sisters] can be injured, despised, rejected, abused, or in any way offended by us, without at the same time, injuring, despising, and abusing Christ by the wrongs we do," Calvin reminds us. Who is at this table? Here *we* are, acknowledging the unity of the community gathered at this Table, but postponing any decisive action about the real presence of the *whole* body of Christ. We ask who is not at the table and ask forgiveness. We ask for some of that divine maintenance and pray for the repair of our brokenness. We hold out our hand.

"This is the Lord's table."

The calling of the church is to turn the tables on the belief that this is our table and that the invitation is ours to issue—whether those who preside or serve or partake. It is the bread we are called to break, not the essential unity of the body of Christ. The calling of the church is to turn the tables on empty ritual, and through an embrace of both mystery and understanding take what happens at this table to the tables of our boardrooms and classrooms and kitchens and committees and work places . . . so that the love and peace and concord of Jesus Christ is present, there, too.

Church happens at tables. We invite you to our common dining-room tables each Wednesday evening during Lent: to break bread together with a simple supper at round tables, building community, and to break bread together in the Lord's Supper at his Table, celebrating Communion. Saint Augustine says that in all that breaking, there is a sacred bonding. Christ, "common to all," making all of us one.

"*This* is the Lord's table. Our Savior invites those who trust him to share the feast which he has prepared."

Amen.

ACKNOWLEDGMENTS:

John Calvin, *Institutes of the Christian Religion*, ed. John T. MacNeill, trans. Ford Lewis Battles (Philadelphia: Westminster Press, 1960).
James F. White, *Introduction to Christian Worship* (Nashville: Abingdon Press, 1990).
Howard Rice and James Huffstutler, *Reformed Worship* (Louisville, KY: Geneva Press, 2001).

10

House-Keeping

Veronica R. Goines

Then the LORD said [to Moses], "I have observed the misery of my people who are in Egypt; I have heard their cry on account of their taskmasters. Indeed, I know their sufferings, and I have come down to deliver them from the Egyptians. . . . So come, I will send you to Pharaoh to bring my people, the Israelites, out of Egypt. . . . I will be with you; and this shall be the sign for you that it is I who sent you: when you have brought the people out of Egypt, you shall worship God on this mountain.

Exod. 3:7–8a, 10, 12

The Passover of the Jews was near, and Jesus went up to Jerusalem. In the temple he found people selling cattle, sheep, and doves, and the money changers seated at their tables. Making a whip of cords, he drove all of them out of the temple, both the sheep and the cattle. He also poured out the coins of the money changers and overturned their tables. He told those who were selling the doves, "Take these things out of here! Stop making my Father's house a marketplace!" His disciples remembered that it was written, "Zeal for your house will consume me."

John 2:13–17

*I*n the Holy Scriptures God identifies divine worship as the central theme of human liberation; worship is the evidence of a liberated people. Between chapters 3 and 10 of the book of Exodus, God repeatedly says to Moses: "Tell Pharaoh to let my people go, *so they may worship me.*" Like a refrain: "Tell Pharaoh to let my people go, *so they may worship me.*" Again and again, "Tell Pharaoh to let my people go, *so they may worship me.*"

While worship and liberation are inextricably linked, God anticipates and makes provision for humanity's paradoxical nature in the Ten Commandments. I once heard a mother say to her children, "I brought you into this world, and I can take you out." God states in the Ten Commandments, "I am the Lord, your God, who brought you out of the land of Egypt, out of the house of slavery. You shall have no other gods before me." While, thank God, the mother of those children never executed the second half of her verbal threat, her words made clear that in her home, she was in charge. Similarly, God establishes sovereignty as the basis for divine-human relationship. All of the prohibitions and the commands that follow in Exodus, including the command to "Remember the Sabbath day, and keep it holy," serve to support this existential imperative to divine worship.

It is the consistent witness of Scripture that the sovereign God of the universe has persistently sought relationship with human beings through their worship. Jesus' radical act of cleansing the temple is directly tied to the constancy of God's call to true worship—*God's* call, expressed in our denomination's Great Ends of the Church as "The Maintenance of Divine Worship," the maintenance of the worship of *God*.

In Hebrew, "worship" means "to make images, to serve, to bow down, to prostrate oneself." In Greek it means "to revere, to serve, to wait on, to do obeisance, and to venerate." In antiquity, worship was associated with ritual acts, but the Old Testament prophets, Jesus, and the apostle Paul all reoriented its meaning toward right living, faith, and love. Prayer replaced the sacrificial system of the temple.

The Jerusalem temple was legitimated as the centralized place of worship in the southern kingdom of Judah. Faithful Jews made an annual pilgrimage to the temple in Jerusalem in hopes of one day seeing the long-awaited Messiah. But over the years, the meaning and purpose of temple worship became obscured—hidden under mounds of merchandizing and heaps of injustice. By Jesus' time, as puppets of the Roman regime, the rulers and priests were profiting from the commercialization of the temple. Instead of fulfilling its purpose as the place of divine worship, the temple had become a tool for the systematic oppression of God's people. It no longer accommodated the presence of the Lord.

I moved into my home in May of 1997. My two-car garage was pristine, with three file-size boxes perched against a side wall. That was it: three boxes! Over the years, home furnishings changed, requiring more storage space. My youngest daughter went off to UCLA but regularly returned home with an accumulation of stuff looking for a safe haven. Now, my two-car garage no longer serves its purpose; it has become a one-car garage.

For the past five years, as I've driven in and out of the garage, I have found it increasingly difficult to ignore what looks like a growing landfill attached to my home. But some weeks ago I found myself in that garage moving with energy and intensity equal to the task, breaking down boxes, sorting the charitable donations from the refuge heap. I admire Jesus for accomplishing in one day what will most likely take me months. It's a work in progress. My garage is far from being a temple, but my goal, like that of Jesus, was not destruction but restoration; not rejection but reclamation.

In the Synoptic Gospels, Jesus' cleansing of the temple comes at the end of his ministry on his way to the cross. But in the Fourth Gospel, Jesus begins his ministry with Jerusalem housekeeping. It is the seminal act from which his ministry emerges. In John's account of the cleansing of the temple, we don't encounter the long-ago Jesus of Sunday school literature, a smiling Jesus with a little lamb slung over his shoulder. Rather, here in the Fourth Gospel we meet God incarnate: the God of the exodus who heard the cries of a suffering and oppressed people and who came down to lead the people to freedom through the agency of worship. Jesus, the incarnate God of a new exodus, settles for nothing less than faithfulness in God's house.

A few years ago I was looking for a rug for my dining room. Much to my surprise, I came upon a long-established rug store in the next town, with a big sign in the window that read, "GOING OUT OF BUSINESS SALE." I was so excited that I made a quick left into the parking lot. I said to the owner that I was surprised he was going out of business. He responded, equally surprised, "I'm not!" I was perplexed for a moment, pointing him to the sign in the window. He pointed me back to a sign on a table. "Look closely at the sign," he said, directing my eyes to the tiny lettering I had missed: "Prices lower than GOING OUT OF BUSINESS SALE."

Some years ago I had a conversation with a colleague in ministry who asked me what I was doing that was causing St. Andrew Presbyterian Church to flourish. I said to him, "I'm preaching the gospel." He responded, "No, that can't be it," to which I said, "I'm just loving the people." Again, he insisted, "No, no, it's got to be something else." And before I could say a word, he said, "I hear that healing services are really bringing folk in these days."

The church in North America, with significantly declining membership, desperately attempts to appeal to a consumer-oriented society. With our eyes on the bottom line, in an attempt to get potential members in the door, churches—like the temple in Jesus' day and the rug vendor in ours—engage in various sorts of fraudulent sales.

> There are the *grand opening sales* that entice folks to the newest trends,
>   but peoples' commitment wanes as the newness wears thin.
> There are *50-percent-off sales*, where the price of discipleship is slashed
>   in exchange for warm bodies in the pews.

Of course, the *buy-one-get-one-free sale* assures churchgoers that they
will always receive more than they give.

Nearly everyone loves a *swap-meet sale*, where the church expends its
time and energy haggling over items of little or no value.

There are *silent-auction sales*, where nothing is asked of God's people,
and as little as possible is given.

And, if nothing else gets them in the door, there is always the *going-out-
of-business-sale*, where anything and everything goes.

Zan Holmes, in his sermon "Are We for Real?" relates a story of a young
man who was seen leaving a church before the worship service was over. An
usher said to him, "Are you leaving the church?" He said, "No. I'm not leaving the church; I'm looking for it."

I was surprised that the rug vendor felt the need to mislead people into
his establishment, given the array of beautiful Persian rugs he sold. Instead
of working as he intended, his tactics caused me, like the young man in the
story, to question the value of his product and sent me in search of the authentic. Do we, the church, believe in the One we proclaim? When strangers enter
the church doors, do they experience authentic, life-giving, soul-saving, lib-
erating worship, or do they leave still seeking?

Every now and then Jesus passes through the doors of the church on a
cleaning spree. His actions often shake our communities at their core. When
Jesus keeps house, it's not pretty. The stubbornness of the strongholds that
bind us is met by the intensity of his redemptive love. Jesus sweeps and
cleans. Sometimes everything is laid bare, pulled out from every closet and
junk drawer; even the garage is fair game. We are sure that we will not sur-
vive. We are certain that all hell is breaking out, but in truth, heaven's breaking in.

In his book on coaching, Rob Voyle reflects on the teachings of psychologist and author Stephen Gilligan:

> Gilligan describes compassion as having three primal energies or faces:
> Tenderness, Fierceness, and Mischievousness. Using this tri-fold under-
> standing of compassion, we can see how the great spiritual leaders were
> being compassionate with those they encountered and how their actions
> resulted in transformation.

Voyle goes on to say, "We are to be tender in the face of pain, mischievous
in the face of resistance, and fierce in the face of injustice."

The blatant practices of injustice witnessed by Jesus did not call for ten-
derness, nor did they warrant mischievousness. In an act of radical interven-
tion, Jesus moves with swift fierceness in the temple. He cleans house. He

removes all that lies in the way of divine intent and true identity for the place and people of God. Jesus does not abandon the temple but cleanses and transforms it so that he can inhabit it, identify his own body with it, and teach and abide there. He removes every obstacle, even the residue of idolatry, which is nothing more than slavery; he eradicates all that obscures the reign of God. With every gesture he says,

> Let my people go, so they may worship me.
> Let my people go, so they may worship me.
> Let my people go, so they may worship me.

The cleansing of the temple was a redemptive act, a reclaiming of divine space for the maintenance of divine worship.

ACKNOWLEDGMENTS:

Zan Holmes, "Are We for Real?" in *Power in the Pulpit: How America's Most Effective Black Preachers Prepare Their Sermons*, ed. Cleophas J. LaRue (Louisville, KY: Westminster John Knox Press, 2002).

Robert J. Voyle, *Foundations of Appreciative Inquiry, Transformational Coaching and Consultation* (Hillsboro, OR: Clergy Leadership Institute, 2006).

11

Justice and Worship

Mark Labberton

Woe to you who long for the day of the LORD!
  Why do you long for the day of the LORD?
That day will be darkness, not light.
  It will be as though a man fled from a lion only to meet a bear,
  as though he entered his house and rested his hand on the wall
  only to have a snake bite him.
Will not the day of the LORD be darkness, not light—
  pitch-dark, without a ray of brightness?

"I hate, I despise your religious festivals;
  I cannot stand your assemblies.
Even though you bring me burnt offerings and grain offerings,
  I will not accept them.
Though you bring choice fellowship offerings,
  I will have no regard for them.
Away with the noise of your songs!
  I will not listen to the music of your harps.
But let justice roll on like a river,
  righteousness like a never-failing stream!"
                                                    Amos 5:18–24 TNIV

*T*he Old Testament book of Amos was written just prior to what would ulti-mately unfold as one of the great crisis moments in Israel's history—when the people of God were sent into exile in a foreign land. So God sent Amos and other prophets to warn the people of God that he was holding their lives to account. Their lives of worship and their everyday lives were being mea-sured by God and were found profoundly wanting.

The Day of the Lord

God is saying over and over again through Amos and the other prophets, "Listen to me. It really matters how you live in the world, how you profess and enact your faith. There is such dissonance between what you profess and what you do that you must be called to account." The discipline that God will bring Israel is going to be the discipline of exile—conquest and captivity by their worst enemies, the Babylonians. Israel was put into the subjugation of that kind of rule in order to discipline them and call them into a process of reformation. God takes the lives of the Israelites seriously, and he also takes our lives that seriously.

The prophet cries out, "Woe to you who long for the day of the Lord!" What Amos is referring to is Israel's grand sense that the hope they were holding out for would be contained in the gift God had promised, called the "Day of the Lord." They expected this to be the day Israel's history would be brought to its culminating point, and the full theocratic rule of God through and for Israel would be established. Israel would be God's people not just in a spiritual and theological sense but also in a geopolitical sense. On the Day of the Lord, everything would finally be made right.

But the prophet Amos questions why Israel would look forward to this day because the day isn't going to bring them the benefits they think it will. What will come with the Day of the Lord is a righteous and holy God who is going to move in among Israel. And as God moves in among them acts of judgment are going to occur. This is extraordinary language. The Day of the Lord will be darkness, not light, as if someone fled from a lion only to run into a bear, as if someone wearily rested against an ancient wall and was bitten by a snake concealed in a crack.

In other words, everywhere Israel is going to turn, there will be accountability and there will be consequences. Everything the people have done has been measured, and it will bring darkness, not light. No wonder Amos and so many of the other prophets reflected on how painful it was to deliver such a message—how much the call to be a prophet was, at its core, a call to suffer. The prophets entered into the suffering of God for the people of Israel who so failed to live the life to which God called them.

Righteousness and Justice

"Righteousness" and "justice" in the Old Testament are translations of the same Hebrew word: *tsedek*. The context principally determines which

English word is the better translation. The reason is that righteousness and justice are, biblically, depictions of relationship.

Righteousness is a representation of a right relationship with God in which the moral character of believers, the way we are following God and the way we are living in the world, looks like the character of God. Believers are called to be righteous people who demonstrate God's righteousness in the world. A right relationship with God necessitates a right relationship with our neighbor. *Tsedek* also means justice. Unfortunately, in our current usage the word *justice* is principally about a judicial or political form of justice. That is not the primary way *tsedek* is used in the Bible, however. It is first and foremost a relational word, so a just relationship is one that embodies and enacts the character of God toward the person with whom we are relating. Justice is the enactment in ordinary relationships of the dignity, value, and worth of one another. Qualities of character, meaning, and purpose are acknowledged, embodied, and respected in relationship to one another.

Therefore, righteousness and justice are two sides of the same coin. This is why God has called Israel over and over and over again to be people of righteousness and justice. Although they had many worship activities, God says, "I hate, I despise your religious festivals; I cannot stand your assemblies. Even though you bring me burnt offerings and grain offerings, I will not accept them. Though you bring choice fellowship offerings, I will have no regard for them."

In other words, the people could bring everything from the lowest kind of offering—a grain offering—all the way up to a fatted calf offering, but it still didn't matter. The Israelites could try to ramp it up by giving God more, but if, at the core, they were failing to demonstrate the reality of righteousness and justice, then God hated their worship: "Away with the noise of your songs! I will not listen to the music of your harps." The worship God wants is not aesthetic worship or artistic worship; it is not worship with proper liturgical structure. Such forms of worship are not what God longs for most.

What God longs for is the worship of our lives that shows up in righteousness and justice. So forget all the aesthetics; God wants an aesthetic of the heart, not an aesthetic of form. God does not want the beauty of creative imagery, or a precise pattern of language, or a particular kind of music. As valuable and meaningful as these things can be, they are perverse if they are devoid of the heart of righteousness and justice God wants. That is why he says, "I hate them." God rejects these forms of worship because they're barren of the things that matter most.

Worship Wars

What does this text say to us today? Righteousness and justice are defined by the character of God enacted in our lives. It matters how we followers of Jesus handle our money, what our attitudes are, what we do for people who are far away, and what we do for those who are nearby. It encompasses all of this, and more, because all of this is part of the righteousness and justice of God.

In practice, however, the church has decided to wean such things out of the world of worship. We think worship is about a liturgical aesthetic, but Amos shows us it is about a moral aesthetic. Worship is about looking like the God you worship, not finding forms that bring you a sense of comfort and beauty. As valuable as those things are, they only matter if they help us live lives of justice, honoring God through righteous acts in the world.

The American church, for at least the last decade, if not longer, has been involved in what some have called "worship wars." Worship wars have to do with ferocious topics like whether drums will be permitted in sanctuaries, whether drama will be allowed in a service, if video can be used, or if candles are appropriate. In other words, the focus is on the things that really prickle people, causing them to say, "That's not my worship." Believers might think that debates about aesthetics matter with unquestioned ultimacy. If they do, they sit under the judgment of God's word in Amos 5.

Imagination

Our imagination is for a world that is God's world, not a world that is merely the world as we see it today. This is where the language in Amos 5 is so powerful. After all of the words of judgment in this passage, God says, "But let justice roll on like a river and righteousness like a never-ending stream." That is almost a non sequitur given what God has just said. What is the logical connection? The connection is that God has given Amos a vision of righteousness and justice and the imagination to see a world that looks like the world God purposes and longs for. And God wants his people actually to embody this vision within themselves and then enact and share it with others.

God is using Amos to stimulate the imagination of Israel, showing them that the rushing force of God's reality in the world is the establishment of a world of justice and righteousness—a world in which the righteous, just character of God is the norm rather than the exception. Part of what cripples believers is that we are people who are weakened in our imagination for justice and for righteousness. We live in a world that has bred in us a fear of anything that appears to be empty idealism or naïve political utopianism. Daring to imagine a world of justice can seem to us a flight of fancy. Although throughout generations some people have tried to establish justice and righteousness, there are twenty-seven million slaves in the world today. More people are enslaved now than at any other time in history.

With the world in such a state, how can we dare to have an imagination for justice and righteousness? Isn't it simply the case that injustice is going to thrive in the world we live in? What difference does it really make whether we have an imagination for justice or not? Aren't we just stuck in the world as it is? However, if we break down the twenty-seven million to just one person who is enslaved, it will allow us to imagine a different question: "Could that one person, who has a name, who was created and is loved by God, be treated righteously and find life in a world of justice?"

This was the very thing that captured the imagination of William Wilberforce. In the late eighteenth century he began to realize the world was filled with people living in slavery. His theological perspective enabled him to see that these slaves were people named by God and loved by God, and that God cared deeply about their suffering. So Wilberforce began to call for a process of transformation, ultimately demanding abolition of the British slave trade.

It was an extraordinary decision on his part, to be an outspoken voice for abolition when most like-minded people thought the idea was desirable but unattainable. Theirs was a poverty of imagination, but that didn't stop Wilberforce from imaginatively conceiving of a world in which the reality of abolition could come to be. So for fifty-eight years Wilberforce gave himself to the humanly unimaginable because his imagination was not informed by the circumstances of history or the people around him. His imagination was filled with the heart, compassion, righteousness, and justice of God.

We live in a culture with an impoverished imagination for justice, but the church of Jesus Christ does not appear to be awake to this concern. Our enactment of justice is meant to be a demonstration that we actually worship Jesus. His suffering generates our imagination, giving us the ability to perceive, at a more profound level, something that is not utopian. This perception will change our aesthetics of worship. It will be an aesthetic of standing in painful places rather than merely experiencing liturgical beauty. True worship is going to call us to places of tears, not just places of comfort. True worship is going to engage us in something that transforms the world, not just something that rebalances our inner psyches.

God calls us to such a radical life of worship. May we follow his call. Amen.

12

A Rendezvous with God

K. C. Ptomey Jr.

The LORD said to Moses: Tell the Israelites to take for me an offering; from all whose hearts prompt them to give you shall receive the offering for me. . . . And have them make me a sanctuary, so that I may dwell among them. In accordance with all that I show you concerning the pattern of the tabernacle and all its furniture, so shall you make it.
Exod. 25:1–2, 8–9

Now even the first covenant had regulations for worship and an earthly sanctuary. For a tabernacle was constructed, the first one, in which were the lampstand, the table, and the bread of the Presence; this is called the Holy Place. Behind the second curtain was a tabernacle called the Holy of Holies. In it stood the golden altar of incense and the ark of the covenant overlaid on all sides with gold, in which there were a golden urn holding the manna, and Aaron's rod that budded, and the tablets of the covenant; above it were the cherubim of glory overshadowing the mercy seat. Of these things we cannot speak now in detail.

Such preparations having been made, the priests go continually into the first tabernacle to carry out their ritual duties; but only the high priest goes into the second, and he but once a year, and not without taking the blood that he offers for himself and for the sins committed unintentionally by the people. . . .

But when Christ came as a high priest of the good things that have come, then through the greater and perfect tabernacle (not made with hands, that is, not of this creation) he entered once for all into the Holy Place, not with the blood of goats and calves, but with his own blood. For . . . how much more will the blood of Christ, who through the eternal Spirit offered himself without blemish to God, purify our conscience from dead works to worship the living God!
Heb. 9:1–7, 11–14

*T*he Russians tell a story about the origins of their Orthodox faith. They say that Vladimir, prince of Kiev, while still a pagan, desired to know which was the true religion. So he sent emissaries to explore the variety of religions in the world. They remained unsatisfied until, the story goes, they arrived in Constantinople and went to the great church there—the Hagia Sophia, the Church of Holy Wisdom. Returning to Prince Vladimir they reported, "We knew not whether we were in heaven or on earth, for surely there is no such splendour or beauty anywhere upon the earth. We cannot describe it to you; only this we know, that God dwells there among [human beings], and that their service surpasses the worship of all other places. For we cannot forget that beauty."

One commentator has said that in the worship of Orthodox Christians, heaven comes crashing down to earth. In a sense, that is what is being described in the chapters of the book of Exodus in which all of the details of the tabernacle are depicted. We read only a few verses of chapter 25 this morning, but the details of the construction of the tabernacle and its contents go on and on for about six chapters . . . and then, a little later, it's all repeated. Exodus speaks of how many curtains and of what size the tabernacle shall consist. It details how many loops shall be on each curtain and how the curtains will be fastened together. It tells us about the furniture: the lampstand, the table of the Presence, the golden jar containing the manna, the ark with its tablets of the law, the mercy seat, and the gold cherubim. There is even a recipe for incense that is to be used in the liturgy. And, of course, there is a description of the Holy of Holies—the inner sanctum into which once each year the high priest went to offer a sacrifice for the forgiveness of sin.

It is easy to get lost in the details, but the point seems to be this: an enormous theological shift has occurred. These chapters of Exodus signal a change in the way God is present to Israel. No longer is God remote, up on Mount Sinai, only to be approached by Moses. Now God is among the people. God is in the tabernacle, which is right in the middle of the camp. In other words, God is not far away, God is with us. Old Testament scholar Terrence Fretheim explains that "God is not like the gods who remain at some remove from a messy world . . . uncaring and oblivious to the troubles of the creatures. . . . God comes down [to the people], rather than the people being asked to come to God."

All the care given to the minutiae—the size of the furniture, the type of wood and metal to be used, even the number and location of curtain loops—reflects Israel's understanding that God has come among the people. Therefore, worship can never be careless of times and places. God has entered into history to interact with God's people, who are not only spiritual beings but physical beings as well. So sights and sounds and smells and movement and touch are all part of God's means of coming among God's people.

In the sights and the sounds and the smells and the bells, heaven comes crashing down to earth. God's people can do no less than stand in awe at God's presence and offer to God in gratitude the most beautiful curtains and furniture and golden vessels and sweet incense and lovely song. Worship is no casual meeting. It is an encounter with the Creator of the universe, who in sovereign love chooses to come among us.

In his commentary on Exodus, Walter Brueggemann says that one way to look at these chapters about the details of the tabernacle and its worship is as a guide that God provides human beings for a rendezvous with God. Of course, God can never be captured, confined, or fixed. The biblical view is not that God is at our beck and call. God remains both near to us and far from us. God has chosen to be with us in worship, but it is not our worship that calls God forth. Yet there is a real sense in which we look to the Bible for guidance on how to have a rendezvous with God. It is why we come to worship as well, is it not? We all long for an encounter with God, a relationship with our Creator.

Over the last several years there has been a resurgence of interest in Bible study in our congregation. A number of groups have formed and undertaken a variety of disciplines of study and prayer. Behind the interest in such groups is, I sense, not simply a desire to know more about the Bible (though that is surely part of the motivation) but a desire to deepen the relationship with God.

Barbara Brown Taylor tells of a time when she served as the coordinator of Christian education in a church. People came to her continually asking for more Bible study, so she engaged seminary professors to teach courses. But attendance was not very good. People had been asking for Bible study but didn't come when the classes were offered. Then it dawned on Barbara that "Bible" was a code word for "God." Her parishioners didn't want information about the Bible; they wanted God, an experience of God, a relationship with God.

You remember that old joke about the sign in a Presbyterian church listing two Sunday school classes? The sign showed an arrow pointing in one direction with the caption "This way to a seminar about God" and a second arrow pointing in a different direction with the caption "This way to God." I think most Presbyterians used to go to the seminar *about* God. But things are changing. I've noticed, as Barbara Brown Taylor noticed, that more and more of us are less interested in a seminar about God and more interested in a relationship *with* God.

Some of us feel at loose ends, without direction in life. We aren't sure why we are in this world and what we ought to be doing, and we need God's guidance. Some carry a load of guilt and are seeking forgiveness. Others of us are facing challenges in our personal life or in our work that are formidable and overwhelming, and we need God's comfort and strength.

It's true, isn't it, that we all hunger for access to the Holy? Everybody needs God's help, God's mercy and forgiveness, God's guidance, God's strength.

Certainly the author of the Letter to the Hebrews understands what we all need and long for. But the writer also knows the frustration of the system in which a priest was allowed into the Holy of Holies to offer sacrifices and to mediate God's forgiveness only once each year. And this writer also knows how easy it is for God's people to get wrapped up in the minutiae of worship, giving attention to the tiniest detail, and yet missing the presence of God. This writer gets it, really gets it—people too often wind up in a seminar about God instead of in an encounter with God. This writer knows, as Tom Long says, that if we are to have a living encounter with God, "then what went on inside that tiny back room of the tabernacle once a year with an elite congregation of one needs to happen in the spaciousness of the cosmos, once for all, for the whole of humanity and with a perfect sacrifice."

And so the author of Hebrews declares that in Jesus Christ we have a great high priest as well as the perfect offering for the forgiveness of our sin. In Christ we have one who brings into the world, once and for all, the abiding presence of God . . . and who in his very life, death, and resurrection, tears down the dividing wall that has separated us from God. This is why John can say in the very opening verses of his Gospel that the Word has become flesh and "tabernacles" among us. Our English translations say "lived" among us, but the Greek word John uses means, literally, "tabernacles." Get it? It's an allusion to the astounding theological shift that we first see in the book of Exodus. God is no longer on the mountain, far removed, but among us, in the tabernacle. And now, that tabernacle, that presence of God among us is found in a person, Jesus, the Word made flesh.

This is not to say that we no longer need worship or places of worship. (You know you would never hear me say such a thing!) All of what we do and say in worship in this place is instrumental to our coming into God's comforting, forgiving, challenging, enlivening, energizing presence.

Jesus Christ, the Word made flesh, is at the very center of our worship, and his cross leads us into this space every Lord's Day. In our processional at the opening of worship, the written Word that bears testimony to God's gracious presence among us follows the cross and is placed in the pulpit, symbolic of its supreme value. We infuse our worship with music and gestures and symbols as well as words, even as Israel and the early church did. We use as many sights and sounds and gestures and smells and bells as we can think of as tools to assist us to become open to the God who is with us whenever two or three of us gather in Christ's name.

Just last Friday someone was speaking about the moment in our worship when the liturgist stands at the font and pours the water. He said, "The sound of that water at first seemed odd to me as a part of worship, but now it fills me with a recognition of God's grace that cleanses me of sin and draws me back into relationship with God." Bouncing off of that comment, I began to rehearse in my mind some of the sights and sounds of worship that from time to time have been occasions in which heaven came crashing down into the middle of the liturgy. I thought of the cries and coos of babies that we baptize; of the glorious, heart-lifting voices of the choirs that fill this place with song; of the way in which Polly so artfully weaves together lines from hymns and anthems to transport us from the offering into the doxology. She lifts us from our pews and carries us to the throne of grace, where we offer our doxology, our praise to God. I think of tears streaming down the face of a bride and groom as they stand here in this chancel and make their solemn vows before God. And I think of tears at funerals and, yes, laughter, too, as we remember and give thanks for loved ones who have died and dare to find joy, even in the depths of our grief, because we know a Savior who was dead but now is alive and in whom we, too, shall be raised from death to life.

This is a holy place not because it looks like a church, with a pulpit and a table and a font and a chancel. This is a holy place because of what happens here—funerals and weddings and baptisms and Communion services and senior Sundays and elder ordinations and the soft candlelight on Christmas Eve. Every time we enter this space we are reminded of some of the most important, most fundamentally human and sacred things we do. Every time we gather we remember those moments when God was so very real and close to us, and such memories reaffirm for us that God does keep God's promise to be present when we are gathered in Christ's name.

The Irish speak of certain locations as "thin places"—a mountain, or a particular place on the seashore, or an old church. "Thin places" where, for some strange, mysterious reason, one can find that the veil separating heaven and earth is sheer, thin, so thin that one can almost feel that heaven and earth are joined. Heaven crashes down to earth. A thin place.

There is no magic formula or ritual or phrase that conjures up God's presence. We must be careful not to take too seriously the notion that this, or any place, is the "house of God." God cannot be captured or confined or fixed or "housed." But for gracious reasons known only to God, there are occasions, symbols, words, rituals, and rooms—like this one—that are thin places in which and through which heaven crashes down to earth, God draws near, and we are touched, forgiven, encouraged, strengthened, healed, given hope.

Worship is not a seminar about God; it is an opportunity for a rendezvous with God. Thanks be to God!

Amen.

ACKNOWLEDGMENTS

Timothy Ware, *The Orthodox Church* (New York: Penguin Books, 1964).

Terence E. Fretheim, *Exodus,* Interpretation: A Bible Commentary for Teaching and Preaching (Louisville, KY: Westminster John Knox Press, 1991).

Walter Brueggemann, "Exodus," in *The New Interpreter's Bible* (Nashville: Abingdon Press, 1995–2002).

Thomas G. Long, *Hebrews,* Interpretation: A Bible Commentary for Teaching and Preaching (Louisville, KY: Westminster John Knox Press, 1997).

4 The Preservation of the Truth

13

A Passion for Truth

Peter B. Barnes

*But as for you, continue in what you have learned and become con-
vinced of, because you know those from whom you learned it, and
how from infancy you have known the Holy Scriptures, which are
able to make you wise for salvation through faith in Christ Jesus. All
Scripture is God-breathed and is useful for teaching, rebuking, correcting and training in righteousness, so that all God's people may
be thoroughly equipped for every good work.*

*In the presence of God and of Christ Jesus, who will judge the
living and the dead, and in view of his appearing and his kingdom,
I give you this charge: Preach the word; be prepared in season and
out of season; correct, rebuke and encourage—with great patience
and careful instruction. For the time will come when people will not
put up with sound doctrine. Instead, to suit their own desires, they
will gather around them a great number of teachers to say what their
itching ears want to hear. They will turn their ears away from the
truth and turn aside to myths. But you, keep your head in all situations, endure hardship, do the work of an evangelist, discharge all
the duties of your ministry.*

2 Tim. 3:14–4:5 TNIV

Introduction

Does this scene sound familiar? When my sons were young, two of them
came into the family room, sobbing in pain, each holding a part of his body
that had obviously been struck with some force, and each claiming that it was
the other's fault. Whose word should I believe?

Or take another example from contemporary life. One economist tells us
the recession is going to be short-lived and we'll be coming out of it in about

six months. However, another economist tells us that we're in this for the long haul and it will take at least two years or more before we're going to see much improvement. Whose word do you believe?

Or you hear on the evening news a government official say that Hamas is at fault for the current crisis in the Middle East, but another official says Israel is the cause of the problems. Whose word do you believe?

In the world of dieting, there's the low-carb diet, the low-fat diet, and the flat-belly diet. Then there's the "Sonoma diet," if you're into the wine country of California. And recently I saw that there is a new "Duke diet." I guess it's for smart people who like Duke basketball as much as I do! What's the best way to lose weight? Whose word do you believe?

People today are looking for a sure word, something they can count on, something they can hold onto, something they can believe in. We feel tossed to and fro by the winds of public opinion, by this claim and that claim, and we yearn for something true in which we can place our confidence and trust. Christians believe there *is* something you can count on, and there is a sure word that is worthy of your belief and your confidence. It is the Bible, God's own Word to humanity.

In 2 Timothy, the apostle Paul states very clearly three specific things that relate to a passion for the truth of God's Word—the authority of Scripture, the activity of Scripture, and the application of Scripture.

The Authority of Scripture

Throughout the centuries, men and women have been engaged in a crisis that is more crippling than a Texas tornado, more devastating than the calamity of world hunger, and as far reaching as the crisis of the global economy. It is the crisis of authority. The late Carl F. H. Henry once wrote, "No fact of contemporary Western life is more evident than its growing distrust of final truth and its implacable questioning of any sure word."

"Everything is relative; there are no absolutes," has become the slogan of postmodern society. And when people are asked penetrating questions about values and the deeper meaning of life, the common response is, "Who can know these things for certain?" Basically, the conflict involves a clash over what is truth and whose word is credible.

In the contemporary world there are generally four sources of authority that people look to in establishing truth. The first source to which many people look today is *science*. "Speculative empiricism," as it is called, the systematic gathering of information by the observational method, is the predominant source of truth in the Western world. Statements like "Studies have shown . . ." or "Polls indicate . . ." are reflective of the way that many people base final authority in matters of truth on scientific inquiry, not on statements of belief.

However, at the beginning of the Enlightenment, French physicist and philosopher Blaise Pascal warned that science alone leaves us wanting and vulnerable. He said, "Physical science will not console me for the ignorance of morality in the time of affliction. But the science of ethics will always console me for the ignorance of the physical science."

The second source of authority to which people look today is *cultural norms*. Whatever is normative for society as reflected in films, TV, and other media becomes the accepted authority. Statements such as "I'm the only one who isn't going" or "I'm the only one who doesn't have X" are representative of this viewpoint. We can even see this expressed at the nine-year-old level when a child says, "Everyone at school is wearing this particular brand of shoes. I've just got to have a pair to fit in!"

The third source of authority that people look to today is *subjective feelings*. "I have to do what's right for me" or "How can it be wrong if it feels so right?" is the philosophy of many people today. Situation ethics is an outgrowth of this perspective, for it bases final authority of the rightness or wrongness of an act on the subjective experience and feelings of the individual, not on an objective source of truth regardless of what one feels.

Today we find ourselves in what academics label as a postmodern world. Bill Robinson, president of Whitworth University, has written that absolute truth has been unseated by relative or culture-shaped truth. Subjectivity has arraigned objectivity on charges of being unknowable, unprovable, and certainly unfashionable. The postmodern answer to Pilate's question "What is truth?" comes in the form of a question: "Whose truth?" The late Catholic priest and author Richard John Neuhaus laments,

> Clear thinking about moral truth founders on the rocks of relativism and subjectivism. In a radically individualistic culture, we do not discern and obey what is objectively true. Rather, each of us decides what is "true for me." We *create* truth. This, however, is not really new. . . . It is a way of thinking and acting that began with that unfortunate afternoon in the Garden of Eden and has resulted in herds of independent minds marching toward moral oblivion.

Robinson notes that Pope John Paul II issued his tenth encyclical, *Veritas Splendor* (The Splendor of Truth), in 1993. In it, the pope hailed the elevated importance of freedom as expressed in the fall of the Berlin Wall and the breakup of the Soviet Union. However, the pope also argued that freedom cannot stand alone without collapsing into a kind of license that ends up denying freedom. He said, "Freedom must be ordered to truth." Truth, with all its moral expressions, forms the backbone of freedom. Moral relativism turns out to be an anarchist in a liberator's clothing.

The fourth and final source of authority is *revelation*, a truth that comes to us from outside creation. The word *revelation* means "truth revealed or unveiled." For Christians the Bible serves as the revelation of objective truth from the One who is beyond scientific verification and who is not bound by cultural norms or subjective feelings. Revelation is God's truth freely given to us.

When Jesus was tempted by Satan in the wilderness, he did not counter the devil's temptation to transform stones into loaves of bread with the statement "Studies indicate that it is difficult if not impossible to change the molecular structure of a rock into that of a loaf of bread." He did not answer, "Where I come from it's not right for a Jewish boy to change a rock into bread." He did not say, "Existentially, I don't feel in my heart this would be a right thing for me to do at this time." Rather, the Son of God said, "It is written: 'People do not live on bread alone, but on every word that comes from the mouth of God!'" He appealed to the objective truth of revealed Scripture. It stands written in the Bible.

In his letter to Timothy, Paul makes the unequivocal statement "All Scripture is inspired by God." This is the critical characteristic of the Bible that makes it the only infallible rule in matters of faith and practice. It is objective truth revealed. It is not simply humanity's word; it is God's Word. Why? Because it is inspired by God. The Greek word that is translated "inspired by God" is actually one word that is formed by combining two Greek words— *theos,* which means God, and *pneo,* which means to blow or breathe. Literally, the word means *God-breathed*!

I have a balloon in my hand. It is only as I blow air into the balloon that it begins to take shape and become filled to its fullest measure. It is my breath that enables it to do what it is supposed to do. God breathed into the writers of Scripture to enable the Bible to become the authoritative truth of God.

Someone will quickly object: "Wait a minute! The Bible was written by people over a period of 1600 years in different parts of the world and in different languages." Quite right, and that is the beauty of it. By inspiring the writers of Scripture, the Holy Spirit did not suppress the personality and style of the authors. Rather, He worked through the particular historical setting, educational background, and the personality of each author in communicating His Word to us through the words of people in history.

For example, if you compare Matthew's Gospel with the Gospel of John, you can see that Matthew was writing for a Jewish audience, so on many occa-

sions he quoted an Old Testament passage to show how Jesus was the fulfillment of Old Testament prophecy. John, on the other hand, was writing for a
predominantly Greek audience, so he utilized Greek philosophy's concept of
the Logos to describe how Jesus was the Word of God made flesh, God with us.

Because God chose to speak His Word to us through the words of people,
every book of the Bible has a historical particularity. Each document is con-
ditioned by the language, time, and culture in which it was originally written. And that is what makes discovering God's Word to us such an exciting
adventure! Simply because the Bible was written by human hands doesn't
make it any less inspired by God. It is God's Word in human words.

Our society, now more than ever, needs a sure word that can be trusted. To
the ultimate questions "Who am I?" "Why am I here?" "Where am I going?"
the Bible alone can give authoritative answers and provide the truth that so
many people desperately seek.

The Activity of Scripture

Our passage in 2 Timothy notes five elements of the activity of Scripture.
These are the things God does for us as we give ourselves to the reading and
study of His Holy Word.

The first activity is *bringing others to a saving knowledge of Jesus Christ
as Lord*. Paul writes to Timothy, "from infancy you have known the Holy
Scriptures, which are able to make you wise for salvation through faith in
Christ Jesus." It is in the pages of Scripture that the need for and provision of
salvation is clearly spelled out. It is through the Bible and God's Holy Spirit
that we are made "wise for salvation."

There are countless stories of people who have come to faith simply by
reading the Bible. Augustine, Martin Luther, and other great people of faith
came to Christ simply through the reading and hearing of the Word of God.
A. M. Chirgwin tells the story of a woman in England who worked on the
ward of a children's hospital. She found life futile and meaningless, and she
struggled to find joy. She waded through book after book and philosophy
after philosophy in an attempt to find peace, all to no avail. But she had never
read the Bible, because a friend had convinced her it was full of errors and
could not be true.

One day, a visitor came to the ward with copies of the Gospel of John, and
she persuaded the woman to read a copy. Later, the woman said, "It shone
and glowed with truth, and my whole being responded to it." The words
that finally changed her mind were Jesus' words to Pilate, "For this I was
born, and for this I came into the world, to testify to the truth. Everyone who

belongs to the truth listens to my voice." She listened to that voice, she heard the truth, and she found her Savior.

A second activity of Scripture Paul mentions is *teaching*. He writes, "All Scripture is inspired by God and is useful for teaching." Are you like me? Many times I'll get a new piece of equipment or purchase a new device, and more often than not I'll try to put it together or figure out how it works without reading the owner's manual. After several hours of frustration and confusion, I'll finally sit down and read through the manual to learn how to assemble the thing and learn how it works. I could save myself so much time and effort if I'd just do that in the first place.

My wife Lorie sat next to a man on a flight to Austin recently who was working with his Blackberry PDA as they were taking off. At first, she thought he was being rude and trying to buck the system by not turning it off, but then she sensed he was having a problem with the device. So she asked, "Are you having trouble turning that off?" He answered, "Yes, I am." So Lorie asked two guys across the aisle from her, "Do either of you know how to turn off a Blackberry?" One of them said, "Yeah, first you've got to scroll down, and there's a icon on the right to power it down." Eventually, after a little coaching, Lorie's seatmate was able to turn off his device. How many of us live in frustration and confusion because we refuse to read God's owner's manual, the Bible, and be taught by it?

The third activity Paul writes about is *rebuking*. What Paul means is not that the Bible is valuable for finding fault. Rather, it is valuable for helping a person to see the error of his or her ways and for pointing a person in the right direction. I've got a Garmin GPS device which is helpful to me in finding my way when I drive in an unfamiliar area. Whenever I make a wrong turn, the Garmin is gentle in its rebuke, simply saying, "Recalculating" or "At your earliest convenience, please make a U-turn." Sometimes the Bible isn't that subtle, but it does provide the rebuke we need to hear when we get off God's path.

The fourth activity is *correction*. The meaning of this characteristic of Scripture is that of restoration. The word translated "correcting" is the Greek word *epanorthosin*. It means "restoration to an upright position or to a right state." The root of this Greek word is where we get many of our English words like *orthodontics*. Just as orthodontics is concerned with straightening crooked or irregular teeth, so the Word of God has the ability to straighten and restore crooked and twisted lives.

Over the years I've talked to a number of people in the congregations I've served who have shared with me stories of how God has helped mend their lives and heal the brokenness they have experienced. Are you broken? Does your life need straightening out? Are you exhausted and in need of God's refreshing? Then read the Bible and allow the Holy Spirit to minister to you and straighten out your life.

The final activity Paul lists is *training in righteousness*. The word translated "training in righteousness" originally meant "the rearing of a child," and later it came to mean more generally, "training, learning, and instruction." It is easy for us to see that we need to use the Word of God in training our children in the way they should go, but of equal importance is the fact that you and I as maturing Christians also need to be trained in righteousness. All of us need discipline in our walks with Christ. As the author of Hebrews writes,

> And you have completely forgotten this word of encouragement that addresses you as children? It says,
>
> > "My son, do not make light of the Lord's discipline,
> >   and do not lose heart when he rebukes you,
> > because the Lord disciplines those he loves,
> >   and chastens everyone he accepts as his child."
>
> Endure hardship as discipline; God is treating you as his children. For what children are not disciplined by their father? If you are not disciplined—and everyone undergoes discipline—then you are not legitimate children at all. Moreover, we have all had parents who disciplined us and we respected them for it. How much more should we submit to the Father of spirits and live! Our parents disciplined us for a little while as they thought best; but God disciplines us for our good, that we may share in his holiness. No discipline seems pleasant at the time, but painful. Later on, however, it produces a harvest of righteousness and peace for those who have been trained by it." *(Heb. 12:5–11 TNIV)*

This, then, is the five-fold activity of Scripture that involves making one wise unto salvation, teaching, rebuking, correcting, and training in righteousness.

The Application of Scripture

Bill Robinson has written,

> As Christians we believe in absolutes. Early church councils affirmed the anchors of our faith. Jesus made absolute claims. He said he is the only way to God—a rather incendiary remark in today's pluralistic world. But as Christian leaders our stout defenses against attacks on moral and spiritual absolutes often omit the way in which we embrace these absolutes—by faith. As finite creatures, we cannot know absolutes absolutely. When

Jesus claims to be the only way to the Father, by faith we believe him. It is not an absolute claim we mortals can prove empirically. But evidence supporting the reliability of Scripture, along with witnessing the profound impact of Christ's transforming love, allows us to hold a reason-based faith that Jesus was telling the truth.

By faith we affirm the truth of Scripture, and it is in the study and application of the Word of God that our lives are transformed. It is not enough to study the Bible and be instructed by it. Where the rubber really meets the road is when we begin to apply the Bible to our own lives. We not only need to become familiar with the truths of Scripture; we also need to flesh them out in our lives daily. Head knowledge is not enough; heart knowledge is equally important. This is where the life-changing character of Scripture really begins to take off. In our passage we read about what happens when we apply Scripture: "that all God's people may be thoroughly equipped for every good work." If you and I apply Scripture to our daily lives, we will be equipped for the work of God in the world.

A number of years ago, my wife and I enjoyed a vacation with our family back at Lorie's childhood home in western Pennsylvania. One of the best parts of that visit was spending time with Lorie's then-ninety-four-year-old maternal grandmother, Olive Carlisle, out at her old farmhouse. Grandma Carlisle was a grand Christian lady, full of life and joy, and she always had a kind word and a smile. One year we gave her a large-print edition of the Bible because her eyesight was failing, and to our amazement we found out that since Christmas of that year till the following October, she had read clear through the Bible once, and she was already up to Deuteronomy in her second time around! This woman of God had known the Lord for most of her life, and she had sought to honor him these many years and apply his Word to her life. Even though she had walked with Jesus for many years, she regularly gave herself to the disciplined study of the Word of God.

Many years ago, Karl Barth was in this country giving lectures at a seminary. At one of the lectures someone asked him, "What is the most profound insight that has been revealed to you in your many years of biblical scholarship and study?" Dr. Barth thought for a moment and then leaned over the lectern and said, "Jesus loves me, this I know, for the Bible tells me so."

Conclusion

Last week I talked with a woman in our congregation who told me of her journey to faith and the way she had sought truth from a variety of paths, including Zen Buddhism. She gave herself to the study and practice of Zen and tried to find truth and meaning, but it left her empty and longing for more. It wasn't until she was an adult that she began to explore the truth of Christianity, and her study of the Bible was key in her decision to follow Jesus. God spoke to her through a particular saying of Jesus that finally helped make things clear: "Whoever does not take up their cross and follow me is not worthy of me. Whoever finds their life will lose it, and whoever loses their life for my sake will find it."

She discovered that in her exploration of Zen she was trying to empty herself and become nothing, but the Bible showed her that the purpose of self-denial and emptying oneself is in order to be filled with the Holy Spirit of Christ and become a vessel of God's grace that he can use. It is only as one loses one's life in Christ that one will ultimately find it. This woman read the Bible; she found the truth of God in the Scriptures; and her life has never been the same. The Bible was one of God's primary means of leading her to a saving knowledge of the Lord Jesus and deepening her life in Christ.

How many of us have multiple Bibles sitting on our shelves gathering dust? When was the last time you gave yourself to the serious study of Scripture? And how are you allowing the Bible to inform and guide your daily life as you seek to follow Christ now? Let me encourage you to develop a passion for the truth of the Word of God and see what a transforming work takes place when you submit yourself to the authority, activity, and application of Scripture.

Amen.

ACKNOWLEDGMENTS

Blaise Pascal, *Penses* #67.
Richard John Neuhaus, *First Things* 40, no. 1 (January 1994).
Bill Robinson, *Incarnate Leadership* (Grand Rapids: Zondervan, 2009).

14

Leading in God's Way

Jerry Cannon

> *After the death of Moses the servant of the LORD, the Lord said to Joshua son of Nun, Moses' aide: "Moses my servant is dead. Now then, you and all these people, get ready to cross the Jordan River into the land I am about to give to them—to the Israelites. I will give you every place where you set your foot, as I promised Moses. Your territory will extend from the desert to Lebanon, and from the great river, the Euphrates—all the Hittite country—to the Mediterranean Sea in the west. No one will be able to stand up against you all the days of your life. As I was with Moses, so I will be with you; I will never leave you nor forsake you. Be strong and courageous, because you will lead these people to inherit the land I swore to their ancestors to give them.*
>
> *"Be strong and very courageous. Be careful to obey all the law my servant Moses gave you; do not turn from it to the right or to the left, that you may be successful wherever you go. Keep this Book of the Law always on your lips; meditate on it day and night, so that you may be careful to do everything written in it. Then you will be prosperous and successful. Have I not commanded you? Be strong and courageous. Do not be afraid; do not be discouraged, for the LORD your God will be with you wherever you go."*
>
> *Josh. 1:1–9 TNIV*

Sometimes it's easy to be cocky and pretend to be brave. It's easy to act like you are in charge when in reality somebody else is doing the work. But when you are faced with the call to be courageous, and when you are put on blast with the challenge to lead with strength, it's hard to pretend to be what you ain't.

Let me say it like this:

It's hard to step up to the plate and claim to be a man if you have been acting like a boy.

It's hard to display the qualities of a woman if all you show is the girlish behavior of a child.

It's hard to rise to the occasion and be responsible when you've been acting trifling.

It's hard to be taken seriously when you have been shucking and jiving all your life.

It's hard to be accepted if you have spent all your time setting up road blocks, building stumbling blocks, and just straight up blocking the progress of folk from whom you now need help to get to where you want to go.

For we have often heard, "You can't be what you can't see" and "You can't become what you are not willing to work for." If you look for dirt on folk, you're gonna find dirt, and if you tear folk down, chances are they aren't gonna be real excited about building you up. For how true is the statement that says, "You can't climb the ladder of success dressed in the outfit of failure." And you can't truly lead unless you have spent some time following.

It's a challenge, Y'all, to be the leader, the motivator, the director, and the encourager if you have spent all of your time and all of your energy pulling folk apart and tearing them down. It's a challenge to be a person in charge if your actions are dedicated to bragging about your power and accomplishments and never seeking to help other folk come together. Leadership requires humility, and leadership requires respect. Leadership is a team effort, and true Christian leadership is Spirit driven.

Let me illustrate by sharing the famous story of "The Lion's Tail." Adrian Rogers tells about the man who bragged that he had cut off the tail of a man-eating lion with his pocket knife. Asked why he hadn't cut off the lion's head, the man replied, "Someone had already done that."

You see, if you claim to be all big, bad, and bold, you ought to be able to do something big, bad, and bold. And if your "greatness" is based on the hard work and expense of somebody else, your brag sheet doesn't mean anything because you can't back up with action what your mouth is busy describing. And if you are an active participant in the ministry of God's church, then that invitation to participation comes with a conditional clause of humility—to follow God's will and not your own. In other words, your real contribution will never become authentic until your desires and your motives are one and the same as God's will for life.

My friends, please hear what I'm saying when it comes to being the person that God wants you to be. For I have discovered that if you want to be the person God wants you to be, it's got to be God's way and not your way. I have discovered that in order to be church, and in order to reach the fulfilled purpose of our lives, the only way that it is gonna work is by doing it God's way. (Amen)

As we look at our text, I believe we see that a lesson on "Leadership God's Way" is being taught to Joshua, a lesson on how to be the person God has called him to be and how to lead the way God desires him to lead.

The text tells us that Joshua gets his chance to lead only after serving in the apprentice role under Moses for years. After the death of Moses, the baton is passed to Joshua to lead God's people. Joshua receives an instructional word from the Lord, yet the condition in which he is to operate is full of circumstances that are not all that inviting for a "first officer" to succeed. Joshua is placed into an opportunistic environment for a leader, yet his position is not enviable. Like most seminarians entering their first calls or like most church officers entering leadership for the first time, Joshua follows one who has been serving for a long time. And a new face on an old block takes some getting used to. (Amen)

Can you imagine the fear he felt, having to fill the shoes of Moses? Can you imagine taking the place of a former leader who could speak to God through a burning bush, and the bush doesn't burn up? Can you imagine coming behind a leader who could cast down his rod and have it turn into a snake, and then retrieve it and find it a rod again? Can you imagine being the successor of a man that could stretch out his rod and divide the Red Sea . . . a man that could bring water out of a rock when the people were dying from thirst? Hear me, church, that is hard leadership to follow.

But not only that, Joshua now finds himself as the leader of a group of people known for murmuring, complaining, backstabbing, and backsliding. He is called to lead people wishing they were back in bondage in the hand of their oppressor. (Let me say parenthetically, in the words of one of my mentors, sometimes you can take people out of Egypt, but you can't get the Egypt out of them.)

Church family, hear me with love today because you must know what I'm talking about. Leading people who want to reach a goal, improve their status, and make a contribution to be successful is one thing. But leading people who are cantankerous, negative, and unmotivated is a different kind of challenge all together.

Yet, as implied in the text, God now looks at Joshua and not at the circumstances and says, "You the Man; go lead." For Joshua there are yet things to accomplish in spite of the opposing forces, but "Joshua, you the Man; go lead!" Moses had led the children of Israel out of Egyptian bondage and through many precarious situations, but now there is the "land of promise" still to be claimed, and "Joshua, you the Man; go lead!" The inhabitants of the land still must be defeated and dislodged. The enemies who are now temporary occupants of your blessings are deeply entrenched in their lifestyle, but "Joshua, *you* the Man!" says God. "Joshua, you are the person I have called, trained, and equipped as the one to lead my people."

Church, can you not hear God saying that to you too? You who have made commitments to serve God with all your heart, mind, soul, and strength. "You are the one; go lead!" Is that not what you are hearing?

To you who have prayed diligently night and day for not your will but God's will to be done in your life, God says, "You are the one; go lead!" Is that not the voice that awakes you and calls your attention to service? Church, by the Spirit that draws us to worship, *you* are the person that Joshua was, and *you* are hearing the voice that Joshua heard. God is saying to God's chosen leaders, "You are the persons; you are the vessels; and you are my chosen, so lead in my Way."

And just how does Joshua manage to do this? What does Joshua need in order to fulfill this awesome task? And to be more specific, how do *we* learn from the text and from Joshua in the text? The answer can be seen in three principles:

1. Be strong and courageous.
2. Be obedient to God's command.
3. Become saturated in the Word of God.

Principle 1: Be Strong and Courageous (Verse 6)

What is courage? Courage has several synonyms: bravery, valor, fearlessness, heroism, confidence, nerve. It also has several nicknames: guts, grit, and backbone.

There's one very important thing we need to notice about courage. You will never witness courage in someone who is at ease in ministry. Courage is seen in people who know what it means to have their back up against the wall. . . . It is seen in individuals who know how to work when the odds are against them. . . . It's seen in men and women who know how to work harder when the pressure is on. . . . It's seen in young adults and seniors digging deeper when they have to dodge the flaming arrows of bitterness and schisms. . . . Courage is seen when the pain is intense, the medicine is wearing off, and time is running out.

> We see *courage* in David with his sling shot, getting ready to take his stand against Goliath.
> We see *courage* when Moses stands eye to eye with Pharaoh.
> We see it in Elijah when he challenges the prophets of Baal on Mt. Carmel.
> We see it in Martin Luther King Jr., facing the dogs and water hoses of Bull Conner.
> We see *courage* in Marian Anderson, facing up to the Daughters of the Confederacy who had refused to allow her to sing at Constitution Hall.
> We see it in Althea Gibson and Arthur Ashe, facing down the racism of segregated southern country clubs that wouldn't let them play tennis because their skin wasn't white.
> We see *courage* everyday in mothers and fathers putting their needs aside to meet the needs of their children.
> We see *courage* in volunteers working countless hours to help those who can't help themselves.
> *Courage* can only be seen in the midst of conflict and struggle.

Why did God tell Joshua that he needed to be courageous? What was Joshua going to face that was so difficult that he would need to be brave? Besides being the leader of the nation of Israel, God had given Joshua a project to complete. His first task was to lead his army into Canaan and drive out the people who lived there. Sounds like an easy job, but remember, forty years before this, under Moses' leadership, he had sent twelve spies into the land of Canaan. They came back with stories of giants living in the land who made them look like grasshoppers. When the people heard this they became afraid and refused to enter the land. Now, just because that happened forty years ago, and this was now forty years later, it doesn't mean the giants were gone. No, it meant that the giants were forty years older and forty years bigger! It takes courage to confront your giant of an enemy who has been preparing for you for forty years.

And not only that, there were seven nations living in Canaan, all of them larger and stronger than Israel. By all human standards Joshua was facing an uphill battle. He had every reason to turn and run. That's why God encourages him so many times: *Be strong and courageous.*

And church, here is my question, do you ever feel like you're facing an uphill battle, or as we say, going up the rough side of the mountain? Do you feel like you have "all clubs in a game of spades"? Come on, be honest with me, because I'm sure that there are times in our lives when we're faced with situations that, to our eyes, seem impossible! From illnesses and sickness to diseases and disabilities . . . from broken promises and broken dreams to busted friendships and busted relationships . . . from financial hardships to more month than you got money and the money you got starts acting funny . . . from the loss of a job to loss of loved ones. . . . I'm talking about hardships and hard times.

Then there are the inner conflicts that test our faith, like attacks on our personal integrity . . . like remaining faithful when no one is looking . . . like enduring the sting of loneliness and separation . . . like standing alone when you're misunderstood . . . like attacks that keep you up at night, attacks that lead you to pray when the "old you" really wants to cuss. There are many times in our lives when we need to hear God's command to Joshua, "*Be strong and courageous.*"

But now, please don't miss this, because there's something else we dare not overlook. Even though Joshua and his nation were small in comparison to the enemy, they had somebody on their side that would tip the scales in their favor. Just like Joshua and the nation of Israel, we may see ourselves as small in comparison to the enemy, but we have somebody on our side that is going to tip the scales in our favor.

God's instruction for leadership begins with this: "*Be strong and courageous. For the Lord your God will be with you wherever you go.*" And church, get this footnote: real success is not a matter of strength and courage alone, but strength and courage that comes from the knowledge that God is walking with us.

Don't miss the point! For Joshua to lead the people into the land of Canaan and claim God's promise he must be strong and courageous. They couldn't do like their parents and cousins and neighbors had done a generation ago and complain and refuse to enter the land because of their fear. God doesn't want Joshua and his generation to make the same mistake. And neither should we.

I think we need to apply this principle not only in our personal lives but also in the life of this congregation. It would be very easy for us to look at this congregation with only our human eyes and human understanding and say, "We're just too small and insignificant to have any influence on the city of Charlotte. Let's just do what little we can and be satisfied with that." You know what that kind of statement says? It's a weak excuse for a weak faith. If we are going to lead God's way, the first thing we must do is be strong and courageous, for the Lord our God is with us wherever we go.

Principle 2: Be Obedient
to God's Commands (Verse 7)

Now the next thing we should do is "be careful to obey *all* the law. . . ." It would be convenient if we could pick and choose which of God's words and commandments we would follow and which we found to be too demanding and too harsh.

We all know what it's like to shop for fruit in the grocery store. Do we think that we can shop for the principles of God's law?—"Let's see, I'll take some love. Oh, here's fresh joy, I always like that. Patience? . . . hmmm, sometimes that upsets my stomach. Forgiveness? . . . I'm not in the mood for that today." Church, please note that the law Joshua was given was very detailed, and God expected him to learn it, meditate on it, and apply it.

In the New Testament, Jesus said that there are two commandments that are most important. What are they? Love the Lord your God with all your heart, soul, mind, and strength. Love your neighbor as yourself. Church, we can't love our neighbor if we don't love God, and we definitely can't stay in love with God if we treat our neighbor any old kind of way.

And you know, I find it most interesting that Jesus says "love" and not "like." You've heard me say it many times before—the church falls short oftentimes in fulfilling God's call because we want to *like* people and not *love* them as the Word requires.

Principle 3: Saturation in God's Word (Verse 8)

The final thing this text teaches about leading in God's Way is that it requires you to be soaked and become saturated in the Word of God. It implies that you must "study to show thyself approved." It means that you must stay firm, focused, favorable, and fit when it comes to putting the knowledge of our God into your spirit and your heart.

Moses, the bearer of God's Ten Commandments, was no longer around. The people had the tablets with the laws inscribed on them, but the real question was whether the laws were inscribed in their hearts. Would old behaviors that the commandments addressed be eliminated in the promised land because there was a change and conviction in the heart? Or would there be a police state of unruly law and order due to a lack of faithfulness to God?

The sure way of connecting the law to the heart and connecting the commandments to strong leadership is the saturation method. Saturation in the Word of God is the certain way to know God's truth and lead in God's truth.

Saturation? Think of the head football coach winning the championship football game and being bathed in a bucket of Gatorade. And think of that bath being repeated day after day. Saturation in the truth of God's Word connects law to heart, truth to life.

I once spent an afternoon trying to get my turntable converter to work, without any success. No wonder—I hadn't connected the belt drive to the turntable, a step I only took after finally consulting the instruction manual. I could have saved myself hours of misery if I had simply read the manual at the start, saturating myself in the proper instructions. We make mistakes when we don't read the instruction manual. That same principle is true when it comes to the Christian walk. Many of the mistakes we've made in life could have been avoided if we had saturated ourselves in the truth of God's Word.

One thing that has occurred to me is that ignorance is no excuse for acting stupid. The mistakes I made with my new converter turntable and computer were made in ignorance, but that didn't stop me from suffering the consequences of acting stupid. My ignorance was deliberate, voluntary ignorance. All the information I needed was available to me, but I didn't take advantage, and I paid the price.

When we try to live without consulting God's Word, it is deliberate, voluntary ignorance. But that ignorance will not stop us from suffering the consequences for acting stupid. The wisdom we need is available. In the Christian life, it's not just about reading God's Word occasionally; it's about meditating on its truth and letting God's Word saturate our spirit and shape our lives.

Leadership in God's Way works, but there are no shortcuts. Leadership in God's Way calls us to be strong and courageous. It calls us to be obedient to all of God's commands. It calls us to saturate our spirit and our will with the truth of God's word.

Amen.

ACKNOWLEDGMENTS

Some ideas for this sermon were extracted from "God's Formula for Success," a sermon found on http://www.free-sermons.org.

The three principles were taken from ibid., "God's Formula for Success," but the preaching emphasis and following illustrations are all mine, picked up from life, television, conversations, and old age.

15

Learning to Tell the Truth

Chris Currie

Then they took Jesus from Caiaphas to Pilate's headquarters. It was early in the morning. They themselves did not enter the headquarters, so as to avoid ritual defilement and to be able to eat the Passover. So Pilate went out to them and said, "What accusation do you bring against this man?" They answered, "If this man were not a criminal, we would not have handed him over to you." Pilate said to them, "Take him yourselves and judge him according to your law." The Jews replied, "We are not permitted to put anyone to death." (This was to fulfill what Jesus had said when he indicated the kind of death he was to die.)

Then Pilate entered the headquarters again, summoned Jesus, and asked him, "Are you the King of the Jews?" Jesus answered, "Do you ask this on your own, or did others tell you about me?" Pilate replied, "I am not a Jew, am I? Your own nation and the chief priests have handed you over to me. What have you done?" Jesus answered, "My kingdom is not from this world. If my kingdom were from this world, my followers would be fighting to keep me from being handed over to the Jews. But as it is, my kingdom is not from here." Pilate asked him, "So you are a king?" Jesus answered, "You say that I am a king. For this I was born, and for this I came into the world, to testify to the truth. Everyone who belongs to the truth listens to my voice." Pilate asked him, "What is truth?"

John 18:28–38a

A number of years ago, *The Christian Century* magazine ran a parody of different denominations and their core beliefs, all in good fun. One of our fellow denominations was teased for its insistence that Jesus was a really nice guy whose whole ministry was about love and compassion, that his central message was tolerance and inclusion of everyone, that all he wanted was for each one of us to find our own spiritual path in life . . . and that in spite of all his good intentions, for some mysterious reason he was arrested, crucified, and killed for his efforts.

Why would a nice guy who preached acceptance of everyone, who seemed so completely harmless, threaten anyone? Why would such a man need to be killed? Why would somebody's compassion, or tolerance, or even his love require his crucifixion?

I wonder if Pontius Pilate harbored some of these sentiments. It didn't seem that he had the stomach to crucify Jesus. He certainly didn't seem to be looking for a fight or even a philosophical discussion about truth. And why does Jesus, who never seemed to back away from a confrontation with Pharisees, or Sadducees, or temple leaders seem so restrained and unwilling to save his own life and preserve the truth? Given Jesus' ability to fend off challenges and Pontius Pilate's queasiness about having anything to do with this man, how is it, exactly, that Jesus got himself crucified?

Pontius Pilate only wanted the problem to go away; the temple leaders wanted someone else to take care of it; and the raucous crowds probably could have been persuaded to take another sacrificial lamb. So, why was Jesus crucified?

Perhaps another way to ask the question is, What is it about Jesus that was threatening enough to cause people to want to kill him and shut him up forever? What was it about who he was and what he said that required him to be taken out immediately? If his message was simply one of compassion and being nice to people, what was so controversial? Was a ministry of tolerance and inclusion all that threatening to the principalities and powers of the world?

Standing before the authority of the Roman Empire, before the religious powers, before a world that prefers more comfortable truths or at least more malleable ones, a peasant rabbi from Nazareth declares himself to be the central truth of this world and God's truth about us. Perhaps this truth offends because it is so public, so deeply incarnational, so earthy, so close to us. As Martin Luther put it, the truth did not become a book or a concept or an idea, but a baby crying and spitting up in Mary's arms. Jesus Christ is Truth. Who he is and what he does become the way truth is defined. In him, truth becomes a human life that is lived out and publicly confessed in the presence of sinners, in the presence of the governing authorities, and in the presence of the watching world. In Jesus Christ, all other truths are measured. In him, we also risk confessing him as truth. But why is the particular truth of Jesus Christ so threatening? What makes him so offensive?

In John's Gospel, Jesus talks about truth a lot. Truth becomes flesh in the first chapter of John; the truth sets us free in chapter 8; Jesus declares himself to be the way, the truth, and the life in chapter 14; and here in John 18, just before his own crucifixion and death, Jesus confesses that his major purpose on this earth is to testify to the truth. Could it be that John is not simply leading us to the cross as a tragic end to an otherwise noble life, or as a mysterious accident that came upon an unsuspecting religious leader, but that he is leading us to the cross because it is precisely there, in the cross, that truth is fully revealed?

The cross is not just a botched job or a tragedy that befell an innocent person, but rather the way that God tells the truth—the truth of a solidarity with sinners so deep that God refuses to turn his back on us and our attempts to live apart from the truth, even if it means losing his own human life. The truth about us is not rooted in our own deepest desires and longings and even our own plans, but in Jesus Christ and his cross. That can be hard to swallow.

Dietrich Bonhoeffer writes that to follow Jesus Christ and to be in the presence of Jesus Christ is to be completely exposed before God. Why else do Adam and Eve scramble around to find fig leaves to cover themselves? Bringing everything to light makes us uneasy and fearful. Bonhoeffer reminds us that we sinners "do not like this kind of truthfulness, and [we] resist it with all our might. That is why [we] persecute it and crucify it." We seek to rid the world of Truth forever by crucifying it, and in the very same cross, God reveals to us a love and a faithfulness that embraces us and never abandons us, even as we try to silence God forever. Even in our desperate attempts to silence the truth through the cross, we are also made to apprehend our own radical need for its truth. And only in the cross can we see the full extent of God's own truthfulness.

Earlier this year Fox TV debuted a new reality game show called *The Moment of Truth*. Contestants answer random personal questions while attached to a polygraph. Then, in front of a studio audience, they have to answer some of the same questions, with the polygraph indicating whether or not they are telling the truth. Meanwhile, backstage, in front of another camera, all of America can see the contestants' family and loved ones watching as the polygraph reveals the contestant's truth and lies. At one point or another in the course of the television show, they are humiliated and hurt and ashamed in full view of millions of TV viewers. Who knew that telling the truth could be so sensational!

In a *Christian Century* article about the show, Andrew Root notes that we often think of truth as baring our souls before others, or in the case of this game show, revealing all there is to know about us. Certainly unearthing such "truths" leads to significant drama and humiliation that make for good television, but in the realm of the crucified and risen Lord, are such "revealed truths" really truthful at all?

In the presence of *the* Truth—lodged in the life of the One willing to stand before all our lies, accusations, and betrayals; in the presence of *the* Truth—whose truth bearing and truth telling led him to suffer in our place and on our behalf; in the presence of *Jesus,* trivial game show truths are exposed as lies that destroy the genuine truth between human beings. If Jesus Christ is truth, then telling all there is to know and damaging those closest to us is not truthful after all.

It would be nice if knowing the truth or confessing the truth meant preserving for us some sense of absolute certainty or full disclosure, but our stake in the truth of Jesus Christ seems to work differently. Jesus' own confrontation with Pilate was filled with risk, but it did not lead him to a frantic attempt at self-preservation. Instead, it led him to risk everything for a bunch of people who do not seem to be worth all the trouble. Confessing Jesus Christ as truth is not the same thing as telling everything there is to know about us. Confessing Jesus Christ as truth will not lead us to absolute certainty or keep us above the fray and messiness of the world.

Karl Barth reminds us that confessing the truth of Jesus Christ "will always cause head-shaking among serious people who do not know the seriousness of [our] confession." So even our own timid attempts to confess the truth and follow Jesus Christ are not risk free. But even here, it is not up to us to prove or justify the truth. Without our aid and assistance, the truth goes before us, the truth that is radically revealed in the Savior who hangs from a tree. It is the truth of God's own faithfulness, a truth that refuses to abandon sinners or let us have our way.

Such truth reveals to us a God who is not confined to the affections of our hearts or to some formulaic evidence of our belief, or even to our ability to make him real and believable. In Jesus Christ, God tells the truth from a cross and from beyond the grave. But that's not all. This Lord also refuses to abandon us in our own feeble attempts at bearing witness to his truth ourselves.

> He is the Truth that miraculously draws us to this place Sunday after Sunday.
> He is the Truth that has sunk himself into our lives in such a way that he will not ever let us go.
> He is the Truth that will not let us keep silent but miraculously equips us to sing it, confess it, and engage the world with it.

How else could prisoners like the apostle Paul, and Dietrich Bonhoeffer, and Martin Luther King Jr. worship God and sing confidently in the darkness of their prison cells?

When I was in the seventh grade, my father would drop me off in front of my junior high school on his way to work. All of the students assembled right in the front of the school in an open area with benches before the opening bell rang, so no one could be inconspicuous. Everyone coming to school was seen by the entire student body as we were dropped off. The front right tire of my father's Oldsmobile had a loose ball bearing that squealed at a high, ear-piercing level (perhaps it is embellished a bit in my imagination) so that the eyes of all my peers seemed to be fixed on me as I made my way out of the car. That is not the way any seventh grader wants to be seen by the entire junior high school.

Even small moments like this remind us of our fear of ever veering too far from what conventional wisdom deems normal. But is it really possible to make the truth of Jesus Christ nonthreatening, normal, and inconspicuous? Far from letting us make the truth palatable to the world, this truth has a life of its own that lays hold of us even as we cling to it for dear life. It calls us to live in ways and engage the world in ways we would never dream of on our own. This cross-shaped truth reveals God himself:

> a God whose very life on earth is the barometer of all truth,
> a God whose cross defines real truthfulness,
> a God who speaks the truth from beyond the grave,
> a God who calls us to follow,
> and a God whose life enables us to tell the truth.

Amen.

ACKNOWLEDGMENTS

Dietrich Bonhoeffer, *The Cost of Discipleship* (New York: MacMillan Publishing Co., 1976).
Andrew Root, "If the Truth Were Told," *Christian Century* 125, no. 16 (August 12, 2008).
Karl Barth, *Church Dogmatics*, III/4 (Edinburgh: T. & T. Clark, 1961).
Timothy George, review of *Freedom for Ministry* by Richard John Neuhaus. *First Things* 192, April 2009.

16

My Way or the Highway
or Many Roads to Heaven

Michael L. Lindvall

Hear, O Israel: The LORD is our God, the LORD alone. You shall love the LORD your God with all your heart, and with all your soul, and with all your might. Keep these words that I am commanding you today in your heart. Recite them to your children and talk about them when you are at home and when you are away, when you lie down and when you rise. Bind them as a sign on your hand, fix them as an emblem on your forehead, and write them on the doorposts of your house and on your gates.

Deut. 6:4–9

"Do not let your hearts be troubled. Believe in God, believe also in me. In my Father's house there are many dwelling places. If it were not so, would I have told you that I go to prepare a place for you? And if I go and prepare a place for you, I will come again and will take you to myself, so that where I am, there you may be also. And you know the way to the place where I am going." Thomas said to him, "Lord, we do not know where you are going. How can we know the way?" Jesus said to him, "I am the way, and the truth, and the life. No one comes to the Father except through me. If you know me, you will know my Father also. From now on you do know him and have seen him."

Philip said to him, "Lord, show us the Father, and we will be satisfied." Jesus said to him, "Have I been with you all this time, Philip, and you still do not know me? Whoever has seen me has seen the Father. How can you say, 'Show us the Father'? Do you not believe that I am in the Father and the Father is in me? The words that I say to you I do not speak on my own; but the Father who dwells in me does his works. Believe me that I am in the Father and the Father is in me; but if you do not, then believe me because of the works

*themselves. Very truly, I tell you, the one who believes in me will also
do the works that I do and, in fact, will do greater works than these,
because I am going to the Father. I will do whatever you ask in my
name, so that the Father may be glorified in the Son. If in my name
you ask me for anything, I will do it."*

John 14:1–14

*E*ver since September 11, 2001, there has been a lot of talk about how religiously intolerant some Muslims seem to be. Islam, some of its adherents say, holds the cosmic franchise on religious truth. We click our tolerant post-Enlightenment tongues and shake our broad-minded Western heads.

But if we're honest, Christians have to confess our own history of intolerance. We invented the Crusades, a century of bloody war designed to coerce the people of the Holy Land into our brand of Christianity. And it wasn't just the Middle Ages. There's a strain of intolerance in modern right-wing Christian fundamentalism, Catholic and Protestant alike. In his novel *Mason and Dixon*, Thomas Pyncheon skewers such Christian narrowness in a character he names the "Wolf of Jesus." This "Wolf of Jesus" Pyncheon says, is "sworn to destroy all who seek God without passing through the toll-gate of Jesus."

The likes of medieval crusaders and Pyncheon's Wolf of Jesus often try to find ammunition in the Gospel of John. They're especially attracted by the passage in which Jesus first says, "'I am the way, and the truth, and the life.'" That's the beloved part. Then comes the verse we love less: "'No one comes to the Father except through me.'" We hear those words and imagine that Jesus is saying the only religion with any truth to it is Christianity, that Christianity is the only way to God.

But not so fast. Remember, Jesus speaks these words in AD 30, more or less. It's the night before the crucifixion. *There is no Christianity yet.*

And to whom is Jesus saying these words? Is he addressing an interfaith conference? Hardly. The only people in the room are his followers. What does hang heavy in the air—in fact the only subject anybody is thinking about—is Jesus' impending death. These words are part of Jesus' struggle to make his disciples understand why there is no way around the cross. He is the Way, the Truth, and the Life—and that Way, that Truth, and that Life are about to be made visible in the towering tragedy of the cross and the towering miracle of the resurrection. In context, Jesus' point is that there is no way to the Father except by self-denial, obedience, and trust such as this. The cross is his way, his truth, and ultimately his life. There is no way to show forth the deepest truth about God except through what is about to happen.

So this passage, misunderstood as it often is, is not really a solid proof text for religious exclusivism. Nevertheless, the fact remains that I am specifically a follower of *this* way, *this* truth, *this* life. I am a Christian, and that means that I believe that God has made God known in Jesus Christ. I am not a Muslim or a Buddhist, and not exactly a Jew. I am this, and I am not that. The reality is, of course, that any faith with any real-world traction has to be just that particular. I mean, if it's not concrete, faith dissolves into vague and pious mists. Jesus Christ is God's specificity: a person like me who lived a real life in a real time and real place. In his humanity he articulates the mystery of God in the only vocabulary I understand: human vocabulary. This is, if you will, the "scandal of particularity."

But in a world of a thousand religions, most of them not much interested in Jesus, this scandal of particularity raises the immense question, "What do I say about all those Muslims and Confucianists, Buddhists and Jews, who claim other ways to know about things spiritual?"

Now, there are two *simple* answers to this question. Like most simple answers, both are popular. Like most simple answers, both are tantalizingly tidy. And like most easy answers, they just don't go deep enough.

The first simple answer is popular at the Right end of the Christian spectrum. This answer says that Christianity is the only religion that contains any spiritual truth. Call this the "my way or the highway" answer. According to the "my way or the highway" answer, all non-Christian religions—except maybe Judaism—are false, pure and simple. They are untrue at best and downright demonic at worst.

The other easy answer lies at the other end—the liberal end of the spectrum. With a caveat here and there, this second simple answer declares that all religions say basically the same thing. Peel back surface differences among religions, this view says, and underneath they are all the same at the core. Call this answer the "every way is a highway" answer. This argument is simple enough. There's only one God after all, right? So aren't all religions simply different paths to that one destination? This position is supremely tolerant, spiritually generous, and politically correct.

A Christian who takes this position might say, "*Personally,* I'm a Christian. Jesus may be my way to God, but if you get there with the Buddha or Krishna or Mohammed, more power to you. It's all the same, right?" This answer is very much a child of modern and postmodern relativism and individualism. "Everything is relative," the 1960s decided. Truth is what you make it, postmodernity says. There are no absolutes. Life is like going through a cafeteria line: some folks like the meat loaf; others like the chicken tetrazzini. Some folks like Jesus; others like Buddha. Take your pick. It's all the same. As long as you're tolerant, it's just a matter of personal spiritual preference.

But are these two tidy answers the only choices? Is it either "my way or the highway" or "every way is a highway"? As a preacher, I've got to tell you that there's part of me that wishes I could preach one of these answers to you: short sermon, easy preaching. But I can't. The fact is, our Presbyterian theological heritage—the "Reformed tradition" as it's known—has thought long and hard about this very question. And, too bad for the preacher, it has gone deeper than either of the tidy little answers. It has insisted on a nuanced and more complicated answer. This answer has none of the rhetorical advantages of the religious sound bite. *But it does go deep.*

You probably didn't come here this morning for arm-pit-deep wade into theology. But I tell you, these are huge questions for a lot of people today: "Can I be a convinced Christian and still really respect the faith of my Jewish or Hindu neighbor?" many ask. "Do I have to believe that their religion is all wrong?" "As a Christian, can I say that underneath surface differences, it's all the same thing?"

The nuanced answer of our Reformed tradition holds the two easier answers in tension. In fact, it makes two towering theological affirmations. These two affirmations stand there, stubborn and rock solid, and gaze resolutely at each other through the great mystery of God.

The first is the bottom-line Christian affirmation that our faith is indeed centered in Jesus Christ. I trust in Jesus Christ as my Lord and Savior—no one else. Jesus Christ is the one through whom I encounter God. *His* words, *his* life, *his* death, *his* life again have come to lie at the center of my very being. As Frederick Buechner said, "A Christian is one who points to Christ and says, 'I can't prove a thing, but there is something about his eyes and his voice. There's something about the way he carries his head and his hand, the way he carries his cross—the way he carries me.'" Our tradition is clear that at the heart of the faith is this resolute trust that Jesus Christ is God's self-defining Word.

So when I encounter people who are not Christians and, heaven forbid, we talk religion, what do I say? Should I convert them or listen to them? Do I tell them what I believe? Well, yes I do tell them, if it fits the conversation. But I don't tell them in order to collect their religious scalps. If I tell them, I tell them because it's good news, and you can't always sit on good news. Good news: the living presence of Jesus Christ in my life has lightened and strengthened and directed me in such a profound way that, if the subject fits the conversation, it would be downright selfish not to share it. This is not "I'm right; you're wrong." It's simply, "Let me tell you what I have experienced in Jesus Christ." This is the first towering affirmation.

But as I said, our Reformed tradition has insisted on a second affirmation that is in what you might call "dynamic tension" with this first. Our tradition has also insisted on an idea called "the sovereignty of God," a five-dollar theological phrase that says, bluntly put, God can do whatever God wants to do. If God wants to speak to people through nature, God can do it. In fact, the apostle Paul argues that God has done just that. This idea is called "general revelation" or "natural theology." It says that God has revealed something of divine purposes "generally" "through nature" to all the world, and anybody with eyes and ears might see it and hear it, Jesus or no Jesus.

The sovereignty of God says that if God wants to speak through secular art or pagan philosophy, even other religions, God can perfectly well do so, simply because God is God and God's freedom, God's sovereignty, cannot be bound. The sovereignty of God reminds us that the divine mystery cannot be fully contained in *any* system of thinking. God is bigger than any theology, bigger than any doctrine about God. The church doesn't contain God; God contains the church.

This sounds rather avant, but it is actually very old stuff. One of the great theologians of the early church was Justin Martyr, who in the second century wrote that some pre-Christian philosophers, Socrates, for instance, were in effect Christians even though, obviously, they had never heard of Jesus. They may not have heard of Jesus, Justin said, but they did know sweet reason, and reason is a gift of God. Justin talks a lot about the *logos*, the *Word* or *reason* in the first chapter of John's Gospel. These old philosophers knew about this, he said, even before Jesus. They lived their lives around it, and that made them something like "Christians," even if they didn't know it.

Evangelical theologian Don McCullough, in his book *The Trivialization of God*, uses a fine image to picture the sovereignty of God: "A child at the beach digs a hole in the sand and, with her little bucket, busily sets about transferring the ocean into it. We smile at the grandeur of her ambition, but only because we know she will soon mature beyond such pathetic futility. Any ocean cannot be contained in any hole of any size on any continent. And neither can God be fully contained with any theological system." McCullough goes on to say, "Once the last plank of our theological house has been firmly nailed down, we may discover that the only god we have contained is too trivial to be worth the effort."

So how about my Hindu neighbor and my Jewish sister-in-law and the Buddhist across the hall? Thank goodness the choice is not between "my way or the highway" or "every way is a highway." If you wanted it simple, I'm sorry. God just isn't simple.

But if we keep our eyes on the two towering truths, in tension with each other as they may be, we find this dynamic place toward the center. And here we can be clear about our Christian conviction, on the one hand, *and* be open to those with other convictions, on the other. Yes, Jesus Christ is my Lord and Savior, and none other. But the God this very Jesus mediates to me is a vast God. The God Jesus shows me is sovereign with a capital "S," and such a mysterious divinity can certainly choose to work in ways that lie well beyond of my mortal understanding.

"You can be an expert in many things," quipped that wise Dutch priest Henri Nouwen, "but you cannot be an expert in God."

In the name of the Father and of the Son and of the Holy Spirit. Amen.

ACKNOWLEDGMENTS

Thomas Pyncheon, *Mason and Dixon* (New York: Picador, 1997).
Frederick Buechner, *Wishful Thinking: A Theological ABC*.
Donald W. McCullough, *The Trivialization of God* (Colorado Springs, CO: NavPress, 1995).

5　The Promotion of Social Righteousness

17

Plain Talk from Jesus on Poverty and Wealth

Timothy Hart-Andersen

When the poor and needy seek water,
and there is none
and their tongue is parched with thirst,
I the LORD will answer them,
I the God of Israel will not forsake them.
I will open the rivers on the bare heights,
and fountains in the midst of the valleys;
I will make the wilderness a pool of water,
and the dry land springs of water.
I will put in the wilderness the cedar,
the acacia, the myrtle, and the olive;
I will set in the desert the cypress,
the plane and the pine together,
so that all may see and know,
all may consider and understand,
that the hand of the LORD has done this,
the Holy One of Israel has created it.

Isa. 41:17–20

For he did not despise or abhor the affliction of the afflicted. . . .
The poor shall eat and be satisfied.

Ps. 22:24, 26

Jesus, full of the Holy Spirit, returned from the Jordan and was led
by the Spirit in the wilderness, where for forty days he was tempted
by the devil. He ate nothing at all during those forty days, and when
they were over, he was famished.

Luke 4:1–2

Then he looked up at his disciples and said:
   "Blessed are you who are poor, for yours is the kingdom of God.
   "Blessed are you who are hungry now, for you will be filled.
   "Blessed are you who weep now, for you will laugh.
   "Blessed are you when people hate you, and when they exclude
you, revile you, and defame you on account of the Son of Man.
Rejoice in that day and leap for joy, for surely your reward is great
in heaven; for that is what their ancestors did to the prophets.
   "But woe to you who are rich, for you have received your
consolation,
   "Woe to you who are full now, for you will be hungry.
   "Woe to you who are laughing now, for you will mourn and weep.
   "Woe to you when all speak well of you, for that is what their
ancestors did to the false prophets."

Luke 6:20–26

*T*he ministry of Jesus begins with forty days in the desert. Typically we think of those wilderness days as we do of our Lent—as a time of sacred asceticism, a period of deep prayer and holy wrestling. Luke, however, avoids the temptation to spiritualize the forty days. "Jesus ate nothing at all during those days," he says rather matter-of-factly, "and when they were over, he was famished." If we are not careful we will miss that key perspective-setting phrase in the Gospel: *he was famished.*

After forty days he must have been near death. Jesus begins his ministry as a starving man. Everything else flows from that gnawing hunger, the poverty of the desert. When he goes to the synagogue in Nazareth to deliver his first sermon after those wilderness days, Jesus starts by reading from Isaiah: "The Spirit of the Lord is upon me," Jesus says, "because God has anointed me to bring good news to the poor." I am here, Jesus declares, to say something good, something hopeful, to those who are hungry—and I am one of them. He wastes no time in making it clear that God's chief concern is the life of the poor.

Jesus does not merely invent this view of God's priorities. Long before him, the prophets and poets of the Hebrew people knew that God leaned in this direction. Hear the words of the psalmist: "God did not despise or abhor the affliction of the afflicted. . . . The poor shall eat and be satisfied." Or the words of the prophet: "When the poor and needy seek water, and there is none . . . I the Lord will answer them; I . . . will not forsake them." In Scripture we learn that God is particularly committed to those who are caught in poverty because they are denied the fullness of life. God's intention for humankind is that justice be planted among the people of the earth and take root and flourish, so that people everywhere might know life in all its fullness.

Nearly five hundred years ago, John Calvin wrote, "The poor are chosen to represent God upon the earth." In our time, Peruvian theologian Gustavo Gutiérrez echoes Calvin. "God has a preferential love for the poor," Gutierrez says, "not because they are necessarily better than others, morally or religiously, but simply because they are poor and living in an inhuman situation that is contrary to God's will."

Jesus begins his ministry as someone who knows what it means to be hungry and poor. So it is no surprise that he opens by restating God's solidarity with those who live in poverty. That is the good news he has come to deliver. This view of God's priorities appears through the entire gospel. We see it in Jesus' teaching, in the parables, in the healings, in the miracles, and in the people he calls to follow him. Everything points in the direction of a social order inverted in favor of those on the underside of history.

Some of us can remember when Bob Dylan first sang about the inversion of things as they are:

> The order is
> Rapidly fadin'.
> And the first one now
> Will later be last
> For the times they are a-changin'.

"The way things have always been" does not motivate Jesus. He is interested in the way things might become. And he is willing to die for it.

A member of our congregation recently commented that we spend a lot of time in worship focusing on the reign of God on earth and less time on the life hereafter. I'm not sure if that was a complaint or a compliment, but it is an accurate observation. Because we believe that our redemption has already been secured by the grace of God in Jesus Christ, we do not dwell on what happens in the next life. With Jesus, our first commitment is to life this side of death.

Our Presbyterian *Book of Order* calls that commitment the "promotion of social righteousness" and declares that such work is one of the Six Great Ends of the Church. Social righteousness looks like this: the hungry are fed; the poor are lifted up; the naked are clothed; those caught in poverty are freed to live as God intends for us all to live.

Too often we act as if following Jesus were mostly about getting our religion right, when it is more about getting life right. God's agenda in Jesus—and, therefore, in the church—is not theological correctness or ecclesial perfection. Jesus did not say, "I came that you might have religion and have it in abundance." (Thank goodness!) God sends Jesus so that *life* in all its fullness might break forth on this earth.

It is the vocation of every follower of Jesus—including you and me—and the work of every congregation of Christians—including Westminster—to spend our lives joining with Jesus in moving toward a world where "justice rolls down like water, and righteousness like an ever-flowing stream." That is a high standard for faithful living, but would we want a more casual Christianity? Would we desire a faith that makes no demands of us, that calls for no change in our life commitments, that does not challenge us or the systemic injustice of our time? Would we place any value in a faith that expects little or nothing of us?

Someone once asked Archbishop Oscar Romero of El Salvador to define the gospel. He said, simply, "To defend the poor as our Lord did." Our infelicitous Presbyterian phrase "promotion of social righteousness" is another version of that same gospel cause. It is a radical, far-reaching agenda, and it is ours.

When Jesus declares himself the bearer of good news to the poor, his listeners become incensed. Maybe he sounds blasphemous to them. Perhaps he injects too much politics into their religion. They run him out of town, and he ends up in Capernaum, on the hilly shores of the Sea of Galilee. Luke tells us that Jesus comes down from the heights and stands on a flat place to deliver what will be the defining discourse of his ministry: the Sermon on the Plain. It begins, as we might expect, with a lesson in biblical economics.

In his sermon Jesus offers plain talk about poverty and wealth. His words are not hard to understand. There is little nuance to them. He makes no attempt to water down what he says and make it more palatable with spiritual language. He does not address the "poor in spirit" but simply, the poor. He does not talk about "those who hunger for righteousness" but simply the hungry.

Nor does Jesus speak in the abstract. "Blessed are *you*," he says. He knows that among those listening that day are people living in poverty, and he speaks directly to them. Blessed are *you* who are poor. He knows firsthand the consequences of their poverty—its physical, psychological, and social impact.

He knows that the poor suffer and die from lack of food:

> Blessed are *you* who are hungry now.

He knows that the poor are often filled with despair:

> Blessed are *you* who weep now.

He knows that the poor are forced to live on the margins:

> Blessed are *you* when people hate you, and when they exclude you.

For to *you*, Jesus says, belongs the reign of God, where you will no longer be hungry, where you will no longer weep, where you will no longer be excluded.

Not everyone standing there on the plain listening to Jesus is poor. Neither are all of his disciples. But the rich who want to follow Jesus will be expected to view and to use their wealth in new ways. Levi, for instance, is a tax collector and a man of means. He throws a banquet after Jesus calls him as a disciple, to celebrate his change of direction in life.

Jesus is not against the rich; he is simply saying that God has a particular interest in the poor. Nonetheless, his words are hard for many of us to hear: "Woe to you who are rich," Jesus says. By the standards of the three billion people in the world who live on less than $2.50 a day, that includes all of us. "Woe to you who are full now," he says. From the perspective of the more than twenty-five thousand children in the world under the age of five who will die today from hunger and preventable disease, that includes all of us.

If we hoped that our religion could remain a fundamentally private matter we were mistaken. If it makes us squirm to be brought face to face with our material abundance, then so be it. The gospel is not meant to justify our standard of living. It was and is meant to be heard by the poor as good news; the rest of us can look forward to the stewardship challenge of using our resources for the sake of the reign of God. That will mean living as simply and as generously as we can.

Jesus makes the elimination of poverty—the promotion of social righteousness—a fundamental aim of those who choose to follow him. If we fall on the wealthy side of the equation, Jesus calls us to be in the forefront of the struggle. That is particularly difficult in the midst of an economic recession, when it is hard for many of us to look beyond our own financial anxieties. In these late winter days of 2009 the global economy has entered into a sort of Lenten season of its own—a period of deprivation, penitence, and sacrifice. Unfortunately, it will last longer than the forty days of its liturgical cousin. We are witnessing the darker side of capitalism, when market fluctuations and vulnerabilities in the financial system coincide to create a free fall. All of us are affected, but hard economic times hit hardest at the people to whom Jesus says, "Blessed are you who are poor, for yours is the kingdom of God."

The recession will end—someday—partly by what the government does, partly because the market will kick in, and partly from what you and I do. I certainly don't mean that you and I should rush out to consume madly again; I mean that we must insist on building different values into the economy of the future. Surely there is more to our economic system than merely adding to the wealth of individuals and corporations. Can we not construct a new economy that is profitable while at the same time sustainable and more equitable in the distributions of its benefits?

The obsessive search for ever-increasing financial gain, whether personal or corporate, is no longer viable. Milton Friedman's principle that "a company's only social responsibility is to increase the profit of its shareholders" will need to be replaced with a broader and more balanced view that recognizes the social value in economic activity. Several years ago, Kenneth Mason, then the president of Quaker Oats, said, "Making a profit is no more the purpose of a corporation than getting enough to eat is the purpose of life. Getting enough to eat is a requirement of life; life's purpose, one would hope, is somewhat broader and more challenging. Likewise with business and profit."

The current economic chaos offers an opportunity to put things back together in a way that reflects a new set of priorities whose test is how the least among us are faring, not how much those at the top are earning. The church can help build the new economic order. Of course, people will tell us that we are meddling in political issues. They accused Jesus of the same thing the day he rose to promote social righteousness in his hometown synagogue.

In a sermon preached from this pulpit at the start of the downward cycle in the world economy in the early 1990s, Don Meisel, Westminster's former pastor, said, "We all know that our civilization is in danger, and yet we seem absolutely incapable of dealing with the danger. What we need is something different, something larger. We have to release an elementary sense of justice, the ability to see things as others do, a sense of transcendental responsibility." That is the aim of Jesus in the Beatitudes as Luke presents them—offering a perspective on human need that includes our shared responsibility, individually and systemically, to meet that need. If some are hungry, if some are despairing, if some are living on the margins, if some are impoverished, Jesus calls us to do something about it.

Jesus remembers that he, too, was once desperately hungry. And he gives his life so that we might see the world as God hopes it will be one day: a place where the poor are lifted up, the hungry fed, the weeping comforted, and the excluded welcomed.

Thanks be to God. Amen.

ACKNOWLEDGMENTS

Gustavo Gutiérez, "Song and Deliverance," in *Voices from the Margins* (Maryknoll, NY: Orbis Books, 1991).

Randall Zachman, review of Bonnie Pattison, *Poverty in the Theology of John Calvin*, in *Spiritus* 7, no. 2 (2007).

National Council of the Churches of Christ in the U.S.A.

18

Deepening Disappointment

Elizabeth McGregor Simmons

The wilderness and the dry land shall be glad,
*   the desert shall rejoice and blossom;*
like the crocus it shall blossom abundantly,
*   and rejoice with joy and singing.*
The glory of Lebanon shall be given to it,
*   the majesty of Carmel and Sharon.*
They shall see the glory of the LORD,
*   the majesty of our God.*

Strengthen the weak hands,
*   and make firm the feeble knees.*
Say to those who are of a fearful heart,
*   "Be strong, do not fear!*
Here is your God.
*   He will come with vengeance,*
with terrible recompense.
*   He will come to save you."*

Then the eyes of the blind shall be opened,
*   and the ears of the deaf unstopped;*
then the lame shall leap like a deer,
*   and the tongue of the speechless sing for joy.*
For waters shall break forth in the wilderness,
*   and streams in the desert;*
the burning sand shall become a pool,
*   and the thirsty ground springs of water;*
the haunt of jackals shall become a swamp,
*   grass shall become reeds and rushes.*

A highway shall be there,
  and it shall be called the Holy Way;
the unclean shall not travel on it,
    but it shall be for God's people;
    no traveler, not even fools, shall go astray.
No lion shall be there,
    nor shall any ravenous beasts come up on it;
they shall not be found there,
    but the redeemed shall walk there.
And the ransomed of the LORD shall return,
    and come to Zion with singing;
everlasting joy shall be upon their heads;
    they shall obtain joy and gladness,
    and sorrow and sighing shall flee away.

Isa. 35:1–10

Now when Jesus had finished instructing his twelve disciples, he went on from there to teach and proclaim his message in their cities.
  When John heard in prison what the Messiah was doing, he sent word by his disciples and said to him, "Are you the one who is to come, or are we to wait for another?" Jesus answered them, "Go and tell John what you hear and see: the blind receive their sight, the lame walk, the lepers are cleansed, the deaf hear, the dead are raised, and the poor have good news brought to them. And blessed is anyone who takes no offense at me."

Matt. 11:1–6

*T*oday is the Third Sunday of Advent, and every year someone asks me this question at least once: "What's up with the pink candle?"

Here's your liturgical history lesson for the day. Peter Bower's *Companion to the Book of Common Worship* tells us that Advent evolved during the fourth century as a period of preparation for the coming of Christ as judge, and so its mood was penitential. But in the Middle Ages, the appointed epistle for the Third Sunday of Advent was Philippians 4:4–6, which begins with the Latin word *gaudete*, meaning "rejoice." The penitential mood of Advent was momentarily suspended by the joyous character of the Philippians text. The candle on the Advent wreath for the Third Sunday of Advent, called "Gaudete Sunday" in some traditions, was changed to pink or rose as a sign of brief delight in the midst of the period of fasting that prepared the church for the Christmas feast.

Today we have read two texts. The first, Isaiah. 35:1–10, like Philippians 4:4–6, pulses with joy. The second, Matthew 11:1–6, drips with disappointment. On this Third Sunday of Advent, the church today, as in centuries past, holds the themes of joy and disappointment in tension.

Do you hear what I hear? Do you hear the voices of our culture chorusing, "That's not right!"? You better believe that you hear them. This is the season not for holding joy and disappointment in tension, but rather the season in which the culture presents lovely tableaux of how joyful everybody is . . . or how joyful we *could* be if only we purchased a Mac to replace our silly outdated PC, or were surprised with a Christmas bow-topped Lexus in the driveway or a diamond bracelet from someone who went to Jared's. *Joy . . . Joy . . . Joy* is the culture's unrelenting holiday drumbeat.

The church strives to be more honest than the culture. The church, at least on its better days, the days when it is most faithful, strives to be honest in acknowledging that while joy is at the heart of faith, disappointment resides there too.

When you stop to think about it, there are enormous pressures on the church to be other than honest when it comes to the reality of disappointment in the life of faith. The pressures are not new to our time, for they were felt in the first century as well. It is striking that the early church remembered and preserved in the biblical record so many stories of times when Jesus caused not joy but disappointment. It is particularly striking that the church remembered and told the story of John the Baptist's disappointment with Jesus because John the Baptist's movement was in some sense a competitor of early Christianity. One wouldn't be surprised at all if the first-century Christian community had done what history is wont to do with those who would be competitors, and that is to write them out of the story altogether.

But the church didn't write John the Baptist out of the story. Instead, the church made John the Baptist the spokesperson for all of us. We hear our own questions, our own disappointments, in the question that John, peering out from between the prison bars, asks: "Are you the one who is to come, or shall we look for another?"

Some scholars say that when John asked the question, he was voicing his disappointment that Jesus wasn't an ax-wielding, fire-and-brimstone-breathing messiah, for that was the kind of messiah John thought the world needed, and it broke his heart that Jesus wasn't it. Maybe so.

But I am not convinced. I think that John knew his ancient prophets pretty darn well. I think he was particularly familiar with the prophet Isaiah and Isaiah's vision in chapter 35. Talk about joy! Isaiah says it all. In his vision, social and political language are woven together in a gorgeous tapestry that displays vivid hope for the complete restoration of all creation. *All* of the world's broken places will be made whole by the in-breaking of the glory and majesty of God: flowers will bloom in the desert and abundant streams will water a land parched by drought . . . weak and infirm people will become strong, the blind will see, the deaf will hear, the lame leap like deer, and the speechless will break into song . . . political prisoners will be returned to their homeland, and joy and gladness will replace sorrow and sighing. The scope of this vision and the hopes it expresses are breathtaking! Isaiah's faith in the possibilities of God that undergirds this language is awe inspiring.

Isaiah's hope for the *complete* restoration of goodness and beauty, for the return of joy to *all* people, for the renewal of the *whole* creation, was squeezing John's heart. But when he put his ear to the prison walls, straining to hear what was happening on the outside, what did he hear? When he squinted his eyes and peered out between the prison bars of his cell, what did he see?

Some who were blind were receiving their sight. Yes, it is true. *Some* were, but not *all*. Some who were lame were told by Jesus to "get up and walk," and they did. *Some* did, but not *all*. John's hope was not limited; he looked for all that was broken to be restored when the Messiah came. When it became true only for some, who could blame him for being disappointed, for sending word to Jesus, "Are you the one who is to come, or are we to wait for another?"

Jesus doesn't blame John for asking the question. In response to John's question Jesus draws John more deeply into his disappointed hopes. Jesus pulls John further into his discontent because in being drawn into the depths of his disappointments he is being drawn into a new way of interpreting what he was seeing and hearing. It seems that God can use disappointment to open us up to something new. Our disappointments can open our ears, our eyes, our souls to deep truth and gracious blessing.

What do I mean by this? The best way I know to express what I mean is to tell you about something that occurred right outside the sanctuary last Sunday afternoon. As some of you know, Murray Owen is making a journey into blindness. He has been gracious in inviting the children and youth of our congregation to learn what the journey is like. Not long ago, Murray and his trainer Ernie Landy cooked up some interesting ways of letting our children and youth experience in some small way what it might be like to become blind and to know the hard work that is involved in learning to function when sight is failing.

Last Sunday, Murray invited Ernie, along with Ernie's dog Mikey, to meet with the youth group following the worship service. Some volunteers had prepared chili for lunch, and everybody was having a noisy, exuberant time in the community room eating chili and having fun. I hated to break up the fun for "the program." I felt a little like Scrooge, actually. You know—the fun is over, kids . . . it's time to go *learn* something.

But Murray and Ernie and Ernie's wife Shauna and Mikey were sitting on the brick wall outside the sanctuary, and they had been waiting a long time, so we went. And you know, there was just something about walking out there and being in their presence that calmed us all down. There was still a lot of activity going on in the courtyard. Every now and then, I would notice little kids running around and playing out on the lawn. But the little space outside the sanctuary where we were sitting and talking was a place of peace. Or at least that is how it seemed to me.

Ernie talked some, and the youth group members asked some good questions. Ernie answered them all. He told us about the program of the Guide Dogs of Texas. And the youth group members asked more good questions. Some church members were leaving by the courtyard as they walked toward home, and they were drawn into the atmosphere of peace. And they asked good questions, too. Ernie and Mikey demonstrated how they work together. Some parents began to arrive, because by this time we had gone way over our 1:30 ending. And the parents asked good questions, too.

Later during the week, as I was reading what Jesus said when John's disciples brought word to him that John had asked, "Are you the one who is to come, or are we to wait for another?" I was struck by his reply: "Go and tell John what you hear and see . . . the blind receive their sight."

As I read those words I thought, "You know, Murray is still blind. Ernie is still blind. And what that means is that in a certain sense, the fulfillment of Isaiah's vision of restoration and wholeness for the whole creation still lies out there in the offing. And in this realization, there is disappointment. But at the same time, there is Mikey. And there is the Guide Dogs of Texas organization. And there are Ernie and Mikey showing us how they work together to "see." They answered our questions, and they told us how we could be a part of the work that they do. And all of us who were there last Sunday afternoon went away less blind than we had been before. And in all of this, in the deepening of our disappointment, if you will, there is, by the grace of God, great joy as well.

And, my friends, that is the honest truth about why there is a pink candle in the midst of the penitential season of Advent.

ACKNOWLEDGMENTS

Peter C. Bower, *The Companion to the Book of Common Worship* (Louisville, KY: Geneva Press, 2003).

Douglas R.A. Hare, *Matthew* (Louisville, KY: Westminster John Knox Press, 1993).

Gail R. O'Day, "'The deaf hear; the dead are raised . . .' (Matt. 11:5): Advent as a Season of Eschatological Possibility," *Journal for Preachers* 19, no. 1(1995): 5.

19

He's Crazy!

Joseph D. Small

> *Then Jesus entered a house, and again a crowd gathered, so that he and his disciples were not even able to eat. When his family heard about this, they went to take charge of him, for they said, "He is out of his mind."*
>
> *And the teachers of the law who came down from Jerusalem said, "He is possessed by Beelzebul! By the prince of demons he is driving out demons."*
>
> *So Jesus called them over and began to speak to them in parables: "How can Satan drive out Satan? If a kingdom is divided against itself, that kingdom cannot stand. If a house is divided against itself, that house cannot stand. And if Satan opposes himself and is divided, he cannot stand; his end has come. In fact, no one can enter a strong man's house without first tying him up. Then he can plunder the strong man's house. Truly I tell you, people will be forgiven all their sins and all the blasphemies they utter. But whoever blasphemes against the Holy Spirit will never be forgiven, but is guilty of an eternal sin."*
>
> *He said this because they were saying, "He has an evil spirit."*
>
> *Then Jesus' mother and brothers arrived. Standing outside, they sent someone in to call him. A crowd was sitting around him, and they told him, "Your mother and brothers are outside looking for you."*
>
> *"Who are my mother and brothers?" he asked.*
>
> *Then he looked at those seated in a circle around him and said, "Here are my mother and my brothers! Whoever does God's will is my brother and sister and mother."*
>
> *Mark 3:20–35 TNIV*

*T*here are moments when we wish we could have been there. When we hear about Jesus' time in Galilee and Judea, we sometimes wonder what it would have been like to be there with him, listening to him tell parables, watching him heal the sick, and basking in the glow of his presence. Oh yes, we can read about Jesus in the Gospels, but how much richer it would have been to experience it all firsthand.

There are other times, when doubts assail us, that we wish we could have seen it for ourselves. Did Jesus really heal sick people? Was his teaching really compelling? Did he truly rise from the dead? If we could have been there to see it with our own eyes, we would know for sure. As it is, we have to make do with second- or third-hand reports.

Whether out of romantic visions of time spent with Jesus or out of wrestling with doubts, our wishing that we could have been there overlooks the reaction of the people who actually *were* there: they thought he was crazy!

Do you remember the way Mark tells the story of Jesus' time in the province of Galilee? It all started with Jesus saying the most audacious thing: "God's Way in the world is happening," Jesus proclaimed. "The time has come, so turn yourselves around and believe the good news." Who was he to say such a thing? And then he began to live it out. . . . He healed people and restored them to wholeness: emotionally troubled people, sick people, disabled people, and dying people. He healed them all as a sign of the new thing that God was doing in the world. . . . When his fame as a miracle worker began to spread, he was besieged by people who needed healing, but he said that his real mission was to proclaim the good news to all people. . . . He began to gather a circle of disciples, yet he didn't select impressive people. Instead, he called ordinary folks and even some who were reprehensible. He associated with riffraff, eating and drinking with disreputable people, and in the bargain he offended the respectable and powerful forces in the community. . . . He disregarded community laws and traditions, and he allowed his disciples to break the rules as well, thus enraging religious people wherever he went. What was worse, he told people that their sins were forgiven, acting as if he were God. Worse yet, he even gave his disciples authority to forgive sins.

We are accustomed to hearing these accounts of Jesus' life as inspiring events that brought new life to the world. But we weren't there when it happened. The people who *were* there, who saw and heard it all, responded quite differently.

Jesus' family thought he was crazy. They thought he was mad to make outrageous claims about God and about himself, out of his mind to deliberately offend the religious establishment and risk the wrath of the occupying Romans. His family's concern about Jesus was not confined to whispered regrets. . . they tried to do something about it. Members of Jesus' family tried to grab him and take him home and confine him for his own good. They thought he was crazy.

They weren't the only ones. Religious leaders thought he was crazy, too, although their diagnosis had a more sinister tone. They believed Jesus was possessed by evil forces. How else to account for his bizarre disregard for centuries-old laws? How else to explain his audacity in presuming to do what only God could do: forgive sins?

We don't have early reports of the Roman occupiers' evaluation of Jesus, but the bitter end shows that he must have been under suspicion early in his ministry. How crazy was it to proclaim the kingdom of God in a Roman colony conquered and occupied in the name of Caesar?

Jesus' family loved him, religious leaders despised him, and tyrants suspected him. Yet all agreed that he must be out of his mind. For his part, Jesus responded vigorously to the charge that he was possessed by evil forces. He was *healing* people, he said, restoring them to wholeness. If he were evil, he would be harming people, not helping them. Jesus responded to his family's concerns as well. When they tried a second time to abduct him, he said that his *real* family was all of those who do God's will. Jesus' many parables about the nature of God's reign must have puzzled the Romans while doing nothing to ease their apprehension.

Well, we assume that as time went by, Jesus' family came around. Surely they must have begun to grasp who he was and what he was doing. Surely they must have been drawn into the joy of the good news. We know that most of the religious establishment never did catch on. Their resentment and hatred grew so that, in the end, they gladly participated in his arrest, trial, and execution. And, clearly, the political regime was unwilling to do anything less than eliminate a perceived threat by killing him.

Yet whether people embraced Jesus, or spurned him, or executed him, the reality is that there is a sense in which it *was* all crazy! Who Jesus was and what he did was a wacky departure from all the accepted norms of society and religion. Jesus was no polite philosopher spinning out reasoned essays on ethics; he was a loose cannon who upset the arrangements of an age.

He romped through a world that not only feared disease but saw illness as a symptom of moral failure and so rejected sick people. Jesus didn't reject those who were ill and disabled. Instead, he made them whole, thereby announcing that God was on the side of sufferers. By what he did, Jesus denied that health was a sign of God's favor, and illness, a sign of God's displeasure. He healed people, restoring them to full participation in all of life. Jesus was on the side of sufferers, and that was strange.

He floated through a world that kept meticulous track of right and wrong, rewarding moral people and despising anyone who fell short of the Law's demands. Jesus didn't despise sinners; he forgave them, proclaiming that

God has no interest in burdening people with guilt. He forgave people's sins, setting them free from the past and free for a renewed future, and that was eccentric.

He barged through a world that divided people into categories, that clothed some with respectability and pigeonholed others as outcasts who were beneath the notice of "the right people." Jesus didn't see anyone as an outcast. He sought out the company of traitors, crooks, revolutionaries, and loan sharks, as well as women, children, and even Pharisees, announcing that all were cherished by God. Such openness seemed muddleheaded. He inserted himself into a world that had resigned itself to empire by making compromises with "the way things are" in order to live at ease with political realities. Jesus proclaimed that God alone is Lord, and that God's rule is the ultimate reality in the world.

He rambled through a world that prized order, a world that gave authority only to people with the right qualifications and expected little or nothing from common people. Jesus expected great things of ordinary people, even gathering poor, uneducated folks as disciples and then giving *them* authority to heal diseases, forgive sins, and break down societal barriers of race, class, and gender. Entrusting his mission to ordinary people was not rational.

It was all crazy. None of it made sense. Who Jesus was, what he said, and what he did were incongruous in a world that looked on departures from "the way things are" as loony at best and dangerous at worst. The reaction of Jesus' family and of the religious and political authorities was understandable. It *was* all crazy.

We ought to be able to understand the reaction of many of Jesus' contemporaries because, truth be told, we think it's crazy, too. Oh, we'd never put it that way, but the fact is that we manage to live with Jesus only by domesticating him, rounding off the rough edges, reducing his proclamation to the empty status of soothing reassurances or unattainable ideals.

Jesus offers us healing and wholeness, but we don't really expect God to cure either personal sickness or society's ills. We are put off by so-called faith healing, and we are thoroughly pessimistic when it comes to faith's power to transform injustice in the world. Perhaps more telling, we are uninterested in Christ's power to heal the breaks in our own lives and to bring about real change in who we are and how we live.

We don't trust Jesus' forgiveness of sins either. We hear the words of forgiveness, yet we either continue to carry the burden of the past on our shoulders or we take forgiveness for granted, assuming that we deserve it. Moreover, we are not very good at forgiving others for the real or imagined wrongs they do to us. Perhaps more tellingly, we view confession of sin as an unwarranted intrusion into our good-enough lives even while we continue to nurse grudges against others.

We don't really believe in human openness and the acceptance of others for who they are. We may pay lip service to the theoretical inclusion of anonymous groups of people, but in more personal settings we draw clear distinctions between "our kind of people" and those from whom we keep our distance. We have little confidence in Christ's capacity to free us from the boxes manufactured by our culture, and, what's more, we're not sure we want to be free.

And even though we are here this morning, we expect very little from the church—the community of ordinary people of faith. We don't trust life here to be different and abundant. If we did, I suppose we'd *all* be here, and we'd be inviting everyone we care about to be here with us.

It's all a bit crazy—from embracing lepers to turning the other cheek to forgiving enemies to finding life by losing preoccupation with ourselves. It strikes us as a wildly improbable way to live, a loopy way of life that just isn't practical, or even appealing, in the real world.

There is a sense in which our reservations are understandable. After all, Jesus' way of living got him killed. But before we too easily chalk up Jesus' way of living as appropriate for a messiah but unsuitable for us, we should notice a few small details about the flow of Mark's narrative. After the events narrated in this morning's reading, Mark relates that Jesus kept on doing what got him called "crazy" in the first place: he told parables about God's new Way in the world, performed miracles, healed people, criticized both religious and political authorities, and made outrageous claims about his mission.

The people who witnessed all of this sensed that something significant was going on, but no one was quite sure what it meant. Even those who were intrigued were puzzled: Was this man another John the Baptist? . . . Elijah? . . . One of the prophets? It was Peter who got it right—"You are the Messiah!"—even though he didn't quite understand what it meant.

"*Then*," Mark says, *then* Jesus began to teach them that he would suffer, be rejected, be killed, and rise again. He said all of this quite openly (no doubt confirming the mental health diagnosis of the authorities), calling "the crowd" as well as his disciples and saying to them—and saying to us—"if anyone wants to become my followers, let them deny themselves, take up their cross, and follow me."

And where are we to follow? Where Jesus has already gone and continues to go, of course. As Jesus' followers we, too, are to work for the healing of people who are ill, families that are fractured, ideologies that are blind, social systems that are disabled, and power arrangements that are sick unto death.

We, too, are to place ourselves with those who are pushed to the periphery: refugees, victims of wars, people without jobs, or homes, or hope.

And we, too, are to speak truth to the powers that be, even when the truth is unpopular.

Jesus proclaimed the kingdom of God—God's new Way in the world— in which *social* righteousness—reordered relationships among *all* people— would be the order of things. No more of the tired old "way things are," but new, God-given, Christ-inaugurated, Spirit-powered possibilities for human living. In short, Christ calls us now to embrace the crazy possibility that life in this world can be free and full for all of God's people. Christ calls those of us who want to be his followers to go where he goes, even when efforts for a more just social order seem foolish, or quixotic, or even a bit mad.

We know that following the Lord is never easy, and we have to confess that we hold back as often as not. But the good news in all of this is that Jesus is still crazy enough to retain hope in us. He doesn't abandon us to our cynicism or forsake us in our easy acquiescence to the way things are. Instead, he continues to put irrational faith in us, remaining with us and for us in the outrageous belief that we can hear his word, walk through life as his free men and women, and form communities of faithfulness that call the world to life in God's fullness.

In the name of the Father, and the Son, and the Holy Spirit. Amen.

20

A Vision for the City

Scott Weimer

> *When [Jesus] came to Nazareth, where he had been brought up, he went to the synagogue on the sabbath day, as was his custom. He stood up to read, and the scroll of the prophet Isaiah was given to him. He unrolled the scroll and found the place where it was written:*
>
> > *"The Spirit of the Lord is upon me,*
> > *because he has anointed me to bring good news to the poor.*
> > *He has sent me to proclaim release to the captives*
> > *and recovery of sight to the blind,*
> > *to let the oppressed go free,*
> > *to proclaim the year of the Lord's favor."*
>
> *And he rolled up the scroll, gave it back to the attendant, and sat down. The eyes of all in the synagogue were fixed on him. Then he began to say to them, "Today this scripture has been fulfilled in your hearing,"*
>
> *Luke 4:16–21*

As I rode in the elevator with the search committee to the top of Atlanta's tallest building, I anticipated a joyous last step in the search process. With a rare view high above the bustling metropolis, I was sure we would look out and offer a prayer of thanksgiving for a successful conclusion to the search. Instead, the chair of the committee pointed out the church building far below and asked me a question that stopped me dead in my tracks. He said, "Scott, what is your vision for our congregation in relation to the city?" My heart sank as I realized that I did not have a clue what God wanted the congregation to do in the city.

I actually thought of the words of Jesus in Luke 4:18–19, and I had a strong sense that Jesus had much to say to the question—something about *bringing good news to the poor, release to the captives, recovery of sight to the blind, and letting the oppressed go free.* Regrettably, I didn't really know how to connect those words to a vision for the city, so I responded to the question honestly: "I don't have a vision for the church's role in the city, because I don't really know the city."

I had every reason to believe that my inability to articulate a strong answer to the question would cause the committee to lose interest in me as their final candidate. Mercifully, the questioner said, "You don't need a vision just now. *We* have a vision for the city, and God will give you a vision in due time. Preach the Word and pastor the people, and God will give you a vision in God's time."

Years later those prophetic words are still being fulfilled. God is giving me a vision for the city and for the role of our congregation in realizing that vision. The biblical verses that are at its center are the very same verses that God placed in my heart at the top of the building—the words of Jesus in Luke 4:18–19. And it is true that many members of the church had a vision for the church in the city, and they have shared it with me. Together, we are finding a fresh and exciting direction for what God wants to do in our lives and the lives of the people around us.

All along I knew the basics of Jesus' inaugural sermon, preached at his home synagogue in Nazareth. I knew that this first recorded sermon after his baptism set the tone for his entire mission and ministry. Jesus' words were based on the selected text for the day—Isaiah 61. I knew that these words of Isaiah were not fulfilled in his lifetime and that they anticipated a future time when the messianic age would commence. The sign of this new age would be hope and blessing for the poor and oppressed, grounded in the compassionate heart of God. In preaching on this powerful text, Jesus claims to be the anointed one through whom this new age has dawned upon humanity. "'Today,'" Jesus said, "'this scripture has been fulfilled in your hearing.'" But I didn't know the power of these words for the church in the twenty-first century. I'm just now beginning to understand what these words mean.

A strong case can be made that Jesus' reference to the poor has both a spiritual and economic meaning. Certainly the good news envisioned by Isaiah spoke to the hearts of those who longed for God and who felt lost when cut off from God's presence. They were first intended for the people of Israel who were living in exile in Babylon. They longed to return to Judah, their historic and spiritual home.

In Jesus Christ, the spiritual home for God's people is no longer a geographic location; it is the very presence of Jesus dwelling in the hearts of all who trust in him and follow him. In Jesus Christ, this good news goes out from the people of Israel to all people, just as God's good news once reached the widow at Zarephath in Sidon in the days of Elijah and reached the leper,

Naaman the Syrian, in the days of Elisha. This good news is for all who acknowledge their spiritual poverty and turn to Jesus in repentance and faith.

But the meaning of "poor" in Jesus' proclamation is surely economic as well. Something good must come from God's heart to those who are economically deprived and struggling for life's basic necessities. Throughout Israel's history, the prophets called the people of God to care for the poor. Likewise, Jesus admonishes his followers to give to people in need and to be concerned for their welfare. He warns the rich that it is not easy for them to enter into the kingdom of Heaven. In fact, it is more than "not easy." It is the hardest thing of all. I am increasingly convinced that the material things of this world often distract us from the most important thing of all—knowing God.

A year ago, men in our congregation began a neighborhood Bible study. Because our neighborhood includes homeless people, business professionals, and college students, the Bible study included men from each of these backgrounds. The results have been transformative for everyone. The study begins with a leader giving an interactive reflection on a passage of Scripture. The men then discuss the text in small groups at round tables. All of the men find themselves on common ground in their need for God and in their spiritual hunger for more of God.

Homeless men have profound insights into the meaning of Scripture from their unique perspectives. A homeless man named Walter recently shared how his life had been in ruins as a result of addiction to alcohol and drugs. With the help of God and the support of his friends inside and outside the church, he is finding freedom from his addictions and making progress toward getting a job.

Tim is a highly successful business professional who had never known a homeless person on a personal basis before becoming a part of the Bible study. As a result of making friends with homeless men, he now feels a profound sense of responsibility for helping to create a climate within the business community to help the homeless find employment opportunities.

College students are learning that in many cases the difference between the homeless community and working people comes down to family support and educational opportunities. All of these men affirm their spiritual poverty apart from God. Each week, good news is being proclaimed to the poor—spiritually and economically poor people.

What about *release to the captives?* In the days of Isaiah, the captives were clearly the people of Israel held against their will by the Babylonians. God's grace would ultimately set them free. Little did I know when I first looked down from the high place above the city that people on and around the very corner where our church has been located for over a hundred years were living in modern-day bondage. A few years ago, the mayor's office issued a startling report. Studies from the FBI and the U.S. Department of Health and Human Services indicated that our city was a center for the commercial sexual exploitation of children. In the midst of Atlanta, three corners were named as particularly problematic for the forced prostitution of children seventeen years of age and younger. One of those corners was the very one on which our church sits.

When I preached about this form of modern-day slavery, the congregation responded with a call to action. Older widows in the congregation offered rooms in their homes as safe havens for recovery. Young people begged for opportunities to form rescue teams that would take their passion for justice into the streets. Still others said they had particular gifts in the areas of counseling, law, and organizational development. In partnership with other faith-based groups within the city, the church helped launch a new city-wide ministry called Street GRACE (Galvanizing Resources against Child Exploitation). This ministry has brought together churches and other faith-based organizations that normally would be separated from one another by theological, ethnic, and cultural differences to work for God's justice for the sexually oppressed children of our city. The good news of which Isaiah and Jesus speak is bringing release to modern-day captives on our very corner and throughout our city!

Many within our congregation are coming to a personal knowledge of Jesus' proclamation of *bringing sight to the blind.* Throughout his ministry, Jesus often worked miracles of physical healing, including restoration of sight to the blind. Some in our church have experienced physical healing and have lived full and meaningful lives far beyond the predictions of their doctors.

When Linda was first diagnosed with ovarian cancer, she was given only a few years to live. Linda trusted God, and people around her prayed for her healing; she lived for over fifteen more years. As one of the most inspiring and grace-filled women in our congregation, she brought love and joy to the lives of countless numbers of people of all ages. Even though her cancer eventually led to her too-early death, everyone who knew her acknowledged God's healing and sustaining presence in her life. She was a modern-day example of one within whom Jesus had worked a physical miracle.

The remarkable story of Jesus' restoration of sight to the blind man in John 9 demonstrates that people with physical sight are often spiritually blind to the things of God. Jesus gives sight to a blind man, who immediately bears witness to the one who healed him. But the religious leaders question his healing. They reject the idea that Jesus could be a true man of God because he does not fit their preconceived ideas of how God operates in the world and in the lives of the faithful. Surely a man of God would not heal on the Sabbath day, a clear breaking of the commandment not to heal on the Sabbath. But the blind man only knows what happened to him—once he was blind and now he sees. And it was Jesus who healed him. This story leads me to acknowledge my own spiritual blindness to what others see more clearly than I. God is at work in ways far beyond my ability to comprehend.

Gillian is an elder in our church who has the gift of prophecy, the gift of speaking God's timely word into our community of faith. As she has shared her prophetic insights with the deacons and elders of our church, they are being fulfilled, sometimes in big ways and sometimes in small ways. God has opened my eyes and the eyes of many of our church leaders to recognize the existence of this spiritual gift of prophecy.

Daily, Jesus is opening the spiritual eyes of our congregation. We are all beginning to see that our church's members from over thirty nationalities have much to teach about God's love and grace and mission. They remind everyone of the global dimension of God's mission. In the midst of the economic downturn, men and women from Africa have shared with the rest of us the devastating economic impact in their home countries. As a result of their insights and the strong call of Jesus to speak into human need, our church has chosen not to cut back on our commitments to mission and evangelism. This is an enormous step of faith for a church that invests over 33 percent of its total income on ministries beyond our congregation. We are reducing expenses in other areas, and we are praying that God will continue to enable us to support the ministries that proclaim good news to the poor and oppressed in our city and around the world. We now see the world with eyes that focus on needs far beyond our own immediate personal concerns.

The chair of the church's search committee spoke a prophetic word when he told me that God would give me and the congregation a vision for the church's mission in the city. That vision is becoming clearer. More than ever, we are convinced that Jesus Christ is the answer to the deepest longings of the human heart:

> In Jesus, the spiritually poor from all walks of life are filled with love, forgiveness, and grace.
> In Jesus, the economically poor hear a word of encouragement and hope for a better life.
> In Jesus, people in modern-day slavery are being set free.
> In Jesus, God's people are mobilized to action—to continue what Jesus began!

Amen.

6

The Exhibition of the Kingdom of Heaven to the World

21

Life in the Waiting Room

Tom Are Jr.

Paul, Silvanus, and Timothy,
To the church of the Thessalonians in God the Father and the Lord
Jesus Christ:
    Grace to you, and peace.

    We always give thanks to God for all of you and mention you in
our prayers, constantly remembering before our God and Father
your work of faith and labor of love and steadfastness of hope in
our Lord Jesus Christ. For we know, brothers and sisters beloved
by God, that he has chosen you, because our message of the gospel
came to you not in word only, but also in power and in the Holy Spirit
and with full conviction; just as you know what kind of persons we
proved to be among you for your sake. And you became imitators of
us and of the Lord, for in spite of persecution you received the word
with joy inspired by the Holy Spirit, so that you became an example
to all the believers in Macedonia and in Achaia. For the word of the
Lord has sounded forth from you not only in Macedonia and Achaia,
but in every place your faith in God has become known, so that we
have no need to speak about it. For the people of those regions report
about us what kind of welcome we had among you, and how you
turned from idols, to serve a living and true God, and to wait for his
Son from heaven, whom he raised from the dead—Jesus, who rescues
us from the wrath that is coming.

1 Thess. 1:1–10

From that time Jesus began to proclaim, "Repent, for the kingdom of
heaven has come near."

Matt. 4:17

I don't know what you think of when you think of the kingdom of Heaven. I don't even know what you like to call it: the reign of God, the Holy Commonwealth, the Day of Jesus Christ. Matthew calls it the "kingdom of Heaven." It is not an easy thing to grasp. That's why Jesus was forever teaching his disciples, "The kingdom of Heaven is like . . . ," and then he would talk about seeds and weeds, surprisingly good Samaritans, and lots of feasts.

I don't know what the kingdom of Heaven causes you to think about. Perhaps you think of justice rolling down like waters, like Amos did. Or maybe you think of swords beaten into plowshares, like Isaiah did. You may imagine the hungry being filled with good things, like Mary did, or you may see prostitutes and tax collectors and the poor finding their place at the feasting table, like Jesus did. Or perhaps you think of things more simply—like everyone down at the food pantry busy working crosswords puzzles because all of God's children have enough tonight. Maybe you imagine the guilt of your own life washed away, or the restoration of relationships long withered by apathy or injury.

No matter what our choice of terminology is for the "of Heaven" part, Jesus wants us to remember that this life does not come from us. It is of God. In Jesus, this new life is with us both as presence and promise. The apostle Paul doesn't speak of the kingdom of Heaven, but he does speak of the life of Jesus as presence as well as promise. Because the life of Jesus is still a promise, Paul describes the experience and practice of the Thessalonian church as one of steadfast hope.

Any parent who has taken a trip with children has heard the pleading question from the back seat, "Are we there yet?" When our children were small, every summer my wife and I would pack the kids in the car and travel to North Carolina, an eight-hour trip from our home in Florida. At about the Georgia state line, with seven hours to go, the kids would begin: "Are we there yet?" The question was repeated over and over all through Georgia, so that by the time we reached South Carolina, I simply said, "Yes. We are there." To which they responded, "This is *it*?"

In a more significant fashion, that is the basic question of faith. Are we there yet? Is the life that we know now, the world that we are familiar with now . . . *is this it*? This question has been part of the conversation of the faith from the earliest days of the church. From the moment when Jesus first said, "The kingdom of God, God's holy reign, has come near," the fundamental hope has been that there is an abundant life that we have yet to know. At times, the only hope that the church could muster was hope for a life beyond this life, which is to say that, at times, the church has boiled the gospel down to mean that the sole purpose of Jesus was to get us into heaven. As Richard

Foster says, a more careful reading of the Scriptures reveals that the greater purpose of Jesus was to get heaven into us.

Paul writes that something *has* happened in Thessalonica. This "something" resulted in "a work of faith and labor of love and steadfastness of hope." Paul goes on to say more about the shape of the faith, love, and hope that was the experience and practice of that early Thessalonian community: "You turned to God from idols, to serve a living and true God, and to wait for his Son from heaven."

You *turned* . . . You *serve* . . . You *wait*. These are Paul's verbs to describe the Christian experience: *turn*, *serve*, and *wait*. *Turning* is not a surprising word to describe the experience of Christian faith. To repent is to turn. But turning is not a one-time experience, which may be why Paul speaks of the "work" of faith. *Serving* is a logical word to describe the work of the gospel. There could be nothing more basic to the Christian life than serving God. This also sounds like Paul's praise for their "labor of love."

But what is the significance of *waiting*? Is there anything especially Christian about waiting? In the Christian life, to wait is to hope, and to hope is to wait. To wait is to live in the steadfastness of hope, to live a life that is constantly shaped by hope. To wait is to let every circumstance be shaped by hope. This is what Paul means when he says that the Thessalonians "wait for [God's] Son from heaven."

Like most pastors, I spend time in hospital waiting rooms. Much of what happens in a waiting room is similar to what happens in other places. People drink their morning coffee and read the paper. They make phone calls or tell stories. Sometimes people initiate conversation with total strangers: "How old is she? Twenty-three months? My granddaughter just turned three in October." Much of what happens in hospital waiting rooms are the same things we do every day.

But there is a difference. In the waiting room there is someone on the other side of the door, and that someone defines life in the waiting room. The waiting room knows that on the other side of that door there is someone who is loved and who loves, and that someone shapes what really matters in this room at every moment. In the midst of the storytelling and the newspapers and the crossword puzzles, there is always an eye on the door. When the door opens, everything stops. Everyone looks.

Well, maybe not everyone. Occasionally there is a person who continues talking, so that in the silence that follows the opening of the door you hear, "I just knew he was going to catch that pass," or something like that. People like that think it is just a room. They have no idea that they are in a *waiting* room.

Paul says the church lives in a waiting room. We wait for what God will do next. We wait for the life of Christ to breathe among us. But our waiting is not about sitting around. Our waiting is not simply passing time. Beverly Gaventa captures the character of Christian waiting: "To wait is to expect." The Thessalonians waited. They expected Jesus, who lived and taught and suffered and died and lives again, to show up among them. They waited for the Son of God to appear among them. This hope is not passive. Hope is not a spectator sport. Hope involves the whole life, the whole heart, the whole being.

Several years ago, Shirley came to our house every other Thursday to help with the cleaning. Shirley was wonderful. It's hard to keep everything the way you want it when the kids are going here and there, and parents are working every day, and there are church meetings, and so forth. So Shirley came and spent a few hours every other Thursday cleaning our home. I did not anticipate the change this would mean for my own life. Every other Wednesday my wife and I engaged in the practice of waiting for Shirley. When I came home from church my wife would say, "Could you clean up the kitchen? Shirley is coming tomorrow." Of course, I would say, "But isn't Shirley coming to clean?"

"Yes."

"Well, why do I have to clean the kitchen if Shirley is coming to clean?"

"Now, Tom, how do you expect Shirley to be able to clean up anything if the house is a mess? Get busy."

I have to confess that I never understood why this worked the way it worked, but my testimony is that by the time Wednesday was over, we were both exhausted as we waited for Shirley. That's what Christian waiting is like. Hope is not a spectator sport; it requires full participation in the life that God has promised. N. T. Wright says that hope is about "practicing, in the present, tunes we will sing in God's new world." He is not talking about music; he is speaking of life.

Paul testifies that Jesus Christ interjected hope into history. Ordinary folk, like the church in Thessalonica, began to dream dreams of a new life and a new world. Where do these dreams come from? Our hopes come from Jesus Christ, for in him we have seen something of what will be. In Jesus Christ we not only see the heart of God, but we also see the way God intends humanity to live. So we wait. We wait for the very life of Jesus to reappear among us.

Waiting means that we seek to be honest in a world where misrepresentation and distortion carry little consequence. We seek to be generous in a culture that confuses greatness with the capacity to acquire. We seek to be peaceful in a culture that has placed far too much confidence in the capacity of violence to produce good. Why do we live like this? Because we are waiting. Because we are living towards the promised day of God.

There are moments in all of our lives when we must decide—Will we wait? Will we hope? Will we be shaped by what we have seen in Jesus Christ but have not yet seen in ourselves? But we also have moments that shape us and inspire in us hope, moments when we know that the life of Jesus Christ is real and transforming.

My brother Gene was born with a generous heart but a limited mind. He will never forget my birthday, but he will never read a book, even a children's book. He knows my name, but he calls me, "Brother," or "Bwuddah," as he says. More than anything in the world, Gene wants to drive a car. That's his big goal in life. He's forty-seven years old, and still the greatest desire in his life is to drive a car. Usually it's a red car; sometimes a van. He wants to get his license, stop by the gas station to "filler up," and take a road trip.

We were eating in Shoney's one day because Gene thinks that's fine dining. We ordered the cholesterol plate and talked about the trips he would take. In a moment that was so real that it seemed unreal, he said, "Bwuddah, do you think I'll ever drive that car?" "Yes, Gene," I said. "Yes I do."

He will never drive the car. Not my car. But it's not really about driving for Gene. His question goes much deeper than that. What he was asking is, "Do you believe this is all there is? . . . Are we there yet? . . . Is there a time when all that has gone wrong will be made right? . . . Is there a holy promise that all that has jumped the tracks can be set right, that all that has been broken will be mended, all that is bruised and crushed will be comforted, all that has gone wrong will be set to rights?" What he was asking is, "Do you believe God will be faithful to the promises on which we stake our lives?" To say *yes* is to spend each day looking for signs of God's faithfulness. To say *yes* is to wait for the life of Jesus Christ to show up among us.

I don't know what the kingdom of Heaven causes you to think about. Perhaps you think of justice rolling down like waters, like Amos did. Or maybe you think of swords beaten into plowshares, like Isaiah did. You may imagine the hungry being filled with good things, like Mary did, or you may see prostitutes and tax collectors and the poor finding their place at the feasting table, like Jesus did. However you think about it, whatever you choose to call it, there is nothing our world needs from the church these days more than this: that we live like a people who still have hope in God's kingdom. The world needs us to live like a people who know there is something we are waiting for.

ACKNOWLEDGMENTS

Richard Foster, "Salvation is for Life." *Theology Today* (October 2004).

Beverly Gaventa, *First and Second Thessalonians,* Interpretation: A Bible Commentary for Teaching and Preaching (Louisville, KY: Westminster John Knox Press, 1998).

N. T. Wright, *Simply Christian* (New York: HarperSanFranciso, 2006).

22

Living under Heaven

M. Craig Barnes

When it comes to the book of Revelation, there are two types of Christians—those who really like it and those who are afraid of those who really like it. Actually, everything the Bible says about the future is meant to help us live more faithfully in the present.

> *Then I saw a new heaven and a new earth; for the first heaven and the first earth had passed away, and the sea was no more. And I saw the holy city, the new Jerusalem, coming down out of heaven from God, prepared as a bride adorned for her husband. And I heard a loud voice from the throne saying,*
>
> *"See, the home of God is with mortals.*
> *He will dwell with them;*
> *they will be his peoples,*
> *and God himself will be with them;*
> *he will wipe every tear from their eyes.*
> *Death will be no more;*
> *mourning and crying and pain will be no more,*
> *for the first things have passed away."*
>
> *Rev. 21:1–4*

> *Then the angel showed me the river of the water of life, bright as crystal, flowing from the throne of God and of the Lamb through the middle of the street of the city. On either side of the river is the tree of life with its twelve kinds of fruit, producing its fruit each month; and the leaves of the tree are for the healing of the nations. Nothing accursed will be found there any more. But the throne of God and of the lamb will be in it, and his servants will worship him; they will see his face, and his name will be on their foreheads. And there will be no*

more night; they need no light of lamp or sun, for the Lord God will
be their light, and they will reign forever and ever.

Rev. 22:1–5

Christ's revelation to the Apostle John takes us through a series of horrific images, all depicting the hardest of times filled with great persecution, tribulation, bloody battles, and unimaginable suffering. It is important to know that these were already the conditions of life being experienced by the first-century church when John wrote down his vision. Jerusalem had been ravaged and devastated by Rome, which had also begun to persecute the church. The early Christians were experiencing great tribulation and martyrdom. The emperors Nero, Vespasian, and Domitian could all compete for the title of "Antichrist."

All of the heartache that John and his church witnessed flew in the face of their great hope that soon Jesus would return and establish heaven's kingdom on earth. Jesus had nurtured a passion for it in the hearts of his disciples. He heaped parable after parable on them, trying to describe it. He said the kingdom is like a treasure found, a lost son who returns home, or a great feast where only the unworthy attend. The kingdom is even like falling in love—but with your enemy.

It had been over a generation since Christ planted those dreams and then left, yet promising to come back and make their dreams come true. Since then, things had become quite difficult for the church. With their world crumbling to an end, the first readers of John's apocalypse were certain that Christ and his kingdom would come soon.

For the last two thousand years, scarcely has a generation passed in history that someone hasn't noticed how harsh the world has become and said, "This is it. This is the end of the line for history. Surely Jesus is returning very soon." Some said it when the twentieth-century genocides gave us modern examples of evil antichrists. Others said it when we invented nuclear weapons capable of creating a literal fiery Armageddon. Still others said it when we sank into the Cold War and learned the rhetoric of evil empires. A while ago, when the calendar flipped over into year 2000, those who believe Jesus can only work in round numbers were sure that was when the kingdom of Heaven would come down to earth.

In the words of church historian Martin Marty, the world is always coming to an end. He said that not just to critique the end-times enthusiasts but simply to say, of course the world is always coming to an end. Just as the world of the first century had come to an end, just as the world of the twentieth century had come to an end and died, so does your world come to an end when someone you cherish dies.

When that happens, when you bury a loved one, what you most want to believe is that the end is not the end. You want to believe that there is something else beyond the life we know. You want to believe that Christ has gone to prepare a place for us. In other words, you want to believe in the kingdom of Heaven.

When I am consoling someone in grief over a life that has come to an end, I will often be asked, "What is heaven like?" Not having been there, I am a bit handicapped in responding. But the Bible does tell us some things about heaven. And the most important thing it claims is that heaven exists. A recent *Time Magazine* poll stated that 81 percent of Americans believe in heaven. (It also claimed that only 63 percent of us believe in hell, which is rather convenient.) But our belief in heaven has little to do with the polls.

Some are puzzled that so many would believe in heaven in a scientific era. Others, however, claim that it is the scientists who have the greatest doubts about the notion of a self-contained universe and are now are making intellectual room for heaven. The new discoveries of supernovas, black holes, quarks, and theories of a big bang lead some scientists to wonder if there is not a grand designer of the universe. Speculation about parallel universes, new dimensions, and anomalies in the space-time continuum have even provided a conceptual framework for some to discuss a wholly different realm of existence beyond the end of what we know on earth.

This is all quite interesting, but you are not going to find a lot of support for these speculations in the Bible. No, the basis of the biblical doctrine of the kingdom of Heaven is found in Jesus Christ. "I am the Alpha and Omega," says the Lord, "the first and the last, the beginning and the end." This means that when you get to the end of life, you're not at the end, because Jesus Christ is waiting on the other side of death with eternal life. And when the church gets to the end of its patience, programs, overtures, energy, and even membership, we are not at the end. There is still Jesus Christ and his coming kingdom of Heaven.

This is John's claim as well. He did not write the book of Revelation to speculate about actual events at the end of time but to provide a metaphorical vision that would encourage the believers who faced tribulation and death as they approached what seemed like the end of their time. At the conclusion of his vision, he makes it clear that the home of God will be among mortals. "He will wipe every tear from their eyes. Death will be no more. Mourning and crying and pain will be no more. . . . Nothing accursed will be found there any more. . . . And there will be no more night. . . ." That sure sounds like heaven. That is how the story ends, and it is also how your story can end. If you know that is how the story ends, it changes your perspective on the chapter of the story you're living today.

Here is John's point: If you believe that heaven is waiting up ahead for you, then it is also always above you. Heaven exists not just as a future place to go after you die but also as an inspiration for the life you have today. If you believe Jesus Christ is behind you and ahead of you, then you can certainly believe that he is also above you. This frees you to live under heaven every day of your life. And that will make all of the difference in how you live your life. In fact, it can make a *world* of difference.

There is an old, rather cynical saying that accuses some people of being so heavenly minded that they are no earthly good. But just the opposite is true for the church. We have nothing good to offer the societies of earth without our vision of the kingdom of Heaven.

If you read church history, you will discover that those who did the most to reform the present world believed most strongly in the world to come. This is true of the apostles who sought the conversion of the Roman Empire, the architects of the City of God that inspired society for a thousand years, the English Pietists who abolished Britain's slave trade, the African American pastor who gave the twentieth century a dream of a color-blind society, the nun in Calcutta who taught us to treat the dying with dignity . . . and the list goes on and on. Where did they all find their vision for life in this world? It came from everything Jesus taught us about the kingdom of Heaven. These who made a difference in the world organized their lives vertically, under heaven, and taught us to do the same.

When Protestants speak of saints, we do not stress only these who were role models of piety and mission. Rather we maintain an affinity for the ordinary variety of saints who died believing in the grace of God, in the sacrifice of Jesus Christ for the sins that separate them from heaven, and in the love of God that raises us to a new eternal life.

On this All Saints' Day, we remember our communion with the saints who died in Christ. To history's list of faith-filled heroes you have to add the names of other, ordinary saints you alone know. They shaped and molded your life by exhibiting the kingdom of Heaven on earth. Now they are all in heaven, risen from the dead.

Down here on earth, people who really believe that live differently from others. They make choices more easily because they believe their choices are seldom ultimate. They are much less cautious with life, much more likely to laugh at themselves because they do not believe they are the Alpha and Omega. They are much more likely to care about others because they do not waste time trying to save themselves, and they are much more likely to enjoy life because they know it is a gift from heaven to be savored.

None of the saints in heaven are there as a reward for a life well lived. They are all there because the grace of God raised them from the dead before they died. From the moment of their baptisms they lived as exhibitions of the kingdom of Heaven, participating in Christ's work of bringing heaven onto earth. That's what makes them our saints.

That can be the legacy of your life as well. All the saints who have gone before you are reaching down over the balcony of heaven, and they are encouraging you to lift up your heart. Lift it above your fear of death and loss and tribulation. Lift it up to the risen Savior so that you too may find a sacred vision for making a world of difference in your corner of the earth beneath heaven.

Amen.

23

Do Not Grow Weary

Dan Chun

> *Do not be deceived: God cannot be mocked. People reap what they sow. Those who sow to please their sinful nature, from that nature will reap destruction; those who sow to please the Spirit, from the Spirit will reap eternal life. Let us not become weary in doing good, for at the proper time we will reap a harvest if we do not give up. Therefore, as we have opportunity, let us do good to all people, especially to those who belong to the family of believers.*
>
> *Gal. 6:7–10 TNIV*

*T*he Bible verse for this morning is "Let us not become weary in doing good, for at the proper time we will reap a harvest if we do not give up." So point one is simply this: Do not grow weary in doing good! Do *not* grow weary in doing good! There are times when we tire of doing good, and we want to throw in the towel, but I'm telling you, "*Don't!*" The Bible tells us to *keep on* doing good. I think we all want to be good and to do good, but the challenges of life can wear us down:

It is demanding to make a marriage work and not give up.
It's hard not to take that one drink when you're an alcoholic.
It's tiring to be a parent.
It's not easy to be a teenager.
It's frustrating to communicate with parents.
It's not easy to choose not to have sex outside of marriage.
It's hard to close off the temptations of pornography.
It can be lonely being honest 24/7 in the workplace and not to cut corners.
It's an uphill battle to continually forgive.
It's grueling to live simply within one's financial means.
It's draining to help those in need.

It's daunting to take care of an aging parent.

It's challenging to be honest always and have integrity in all we do.

But we hear the Bible saying, *"DO NOT BE WEARY IN DOING GOOD!"*

My dear, dear friend Pat Taylor, an elder of this church, retired after a long career helping the community through her job at the University of Hawaii and through her work with the Blood Bank of Hawaii. She retired in April as the chair of UH's medical laboratory technology department.

One month later she was diagnosed with cancer. One month after that she suffered a stroke, became paralyzed on her right side, and lost most of her speech. Today she is in a nursing home, and her friends, the deacons, the elders, and our staff minister to her. They visit her regularly. When she can't feed herself, they feed her. Her best friends, Takeyo Saito, Susan Pang, Janet Tamura, and Dr. Ann Catts, are taking care of her apartment and helping with finances. For her birthday two Fridays ago the staff made a big banner for her room and gave gifts.

I have known Pat for nearly thirty years as her friend and pastor. We all love her. We are all trying to help her, but it is hard, because she doesn't remember who we are. She doesn't recognize me, or most of her friends, or the staff. But we love her so much that we will continue to help her the best we can.

A poignant moment came a few days ago when I visited Pat. She used to sing in the choir, and so she and I sang together, "Jesus loves me, this I know; for the Bible tells me so. Yes, Jesus loves me. Yes, Jesus loves me. Yes, Jesus loves me; the Bible tells me so." I cried most of the way home. She has lost the use of some of her limbs, her speech, her memory . . . and yet she knows that Jesus loves her.

All of us have been there. We all have friends, parents, children, or bosses who, for whatever reason, do not or cannot respond to us when we do what is right and good. But know what Scripture calls us to: Do not grow weary in doing good, and don't expect reward or recognition. The reward is in the doing, not in the response of others or in the satisfied memory of what you have done.

Ramona Harris, former first lady of Honolulu and an elder of our church, often danced hula for senior citizens groups. I admired Ramona for doing this. Was she doing it because the people she danced for would say, "Oh, what a nice mayor's wife," or so that people would vote for her husband? No. You see, these senior citizens had Alzheimer's. They wouldn't remember all the times Ramona danced for them. They wouldn't even remember Ramona. And yet she poured love onto them.

Do not become weary in doing good. Why? Well, because it is the right thing to do. But our verse also comes home with this point: "Let us not become weary in doing good, for at the proper time *we will reap a harvest* if we do not give up." The Bible is saying that whenever we do good, what we sow will bring a harvest of blessing. How?

Doing good for others is good for us! It is good for our health, our psyche, and our walk with God. Wanting to do good puts us in a positive and helping spirit.

And, doing good is infectious. It extends an attitude that builds faith in others, builds families, nurtures churches, encourages communities, and sustains the world.

But what kind of harvest do we reap by doing good? What is the fruit of product?

First, by our actions we may lead someone to faith in Christ. Good work becomes a silent ministry in the marketplace, as we share the gospel of Christ through our deeds and not only our words. When we work honestly, act with integrity, and stand up for others, people notice. I will speak at our men's ministry dinner this month, and one of my points will be that the places we work are the mission fields to which God has called us or the parishes God has given us to minister in. All of our fellow employees, all of our customers, are people we can share the love of Jesus with. Imagine—God gives us the mission field and gets our company to pay us to minister!

A second harvest of the fruit of good work is that we can literally save people from hunger or danger or death if we do not grow weary in doing good. As part of my sabbatical I went to Manila in July to meet Gary Haugen, the founder of IJM, the International Justice Mission. IJM is dedicated in the Lord to rescue children who have been sold into illegal child labor and sex slavery or have been victimized by sexual or physical abuse. IJM works with local law enforcement to ensure that criminal justice systems work on behalf of the poor.

The IJM staff and I met with Philippine vice president Noli de Castro to explain what IJM does and how it can work with the government to put away the people who are trafficking children. The Philippine government expressed its strong interest in working with IJM, especially since their own agencies are overworked in trying to put away the perpetrators.

One thing I took away from this trip was an awareness of the deep oppression of evil. The scope of suffering in the world is wide and deep. Learning about corrupt governments, organized crime, abusive parents, sexual abuse, the poverty of opportunity, and the devastation of children made my heart weep. The odds are overwhelming and seem impossible to fight. There is so much evil, and it seemed to me during my sabbatical that it is directed specifically at children—children as young as five years old who are being kidnapped and sold into prostitution, or forced into long hours of labor in sweat shops and beaten by their parents. Some of the children's limbs are purposely cut off or broken so that they can get more money begging. These abused children grow up to become adults geared for a lifetime of prostitution, crime, poverty, and begging.

But then I came to this realization: In the fight against injustice, evil people are depending on good people to give up. So that they can continue to do their horrible work, evil people are depending on good people to grow weary in doing good, to despair, to throw in the towel, and to quit.

International Justice Mission works to rescue children from violent oppression in Southeast Asia, South Asia, Africa, and Latin America. Sometimes IJM may work for months or years to get ready for an operation, dedicating long hours to surveillance and preparing their legal work. Because they don't give up, their arduous planning will eventually lead to a successful operation that may rescue thirty or forty children from the darkness of slavery in a brothel and deliver them to safety and eventually to the light of Jesus.

But get this—sometimes a policeman may tip off the brothel owners and pimps just hours before the rescue operation. The whole case is blown! IJM workers despair! Children remain in slavery! Months of work down the drain!

Seeing such failure happen again and again makes you want to quit. But Philippines IJM director Mia Andal-Castro told me that normally, when one employee feels so down that it makes him or her want to quit, another gets energized and says, "No, we can do it. Don't give up! Don't give up! The children need us to defeat evil!"

Evil bets on the good people quitting and saying, "Forget it." So the way to defeat evil is *not* to quit and *not* to grow weary in doing good—to keep on keeping on. The way to defeat evil is to persevere in doing good together with a community of encouragers. The church is called to be that community.

What is the harvest? It's saving a child who needs someone in this world to tell her that God loves her. It's giving a child a chance to grow up and live a new and healthy life. Our Bible verse says we will reap abundantly at harvest time. If we do not become weary in doing good, there will be a great yield.

Many of the IJM staff are in their twenties and thirties. I am so proud of them. They could have become wealthy lawyers in corporate offices, or well-paid therapists, but they choose to devote themselves to fighting injustice as lawyers, counselors, and social workers for IJM instead.

I joined the IJM staff on a prayer retreat in Manila. Prayer is big for them. In fact, it is mandatory that the first thirty minutes of their time in the office at their desks is to be a personal devotional time. At the retreat, Gary Haugen talked with the staff about humility and how they need to rely on God and one another. As they rely on God and one another, they are able to work with judges and the police to try to save children through bold, courageous raids. As they rely on God and one another, their mission attracts the support of others. The Bill and Melinda Gates Foundation recently gave a grant to IJM; this is amazing because the Gates Foundation normally does not give to evangelical Christian organizations.

Although I have visited IJM in the Philippines, I can't tell you where its offices are because the location must remain hidden, and even then there must be an armed guard outside. Evil would like to put them out of the business of doing good. At least one staff member has already been killed, and several more have been threatened with harm.

You might think to yourself, "There are so many children who need help out there. What can I do?" The United Nations reports that more than a million new children are forced into prostitution every year. *One million!* And so we ask, "What can I do? By saving one—or even thirty—does it really matter?" Well, it surely matters to that one child.

It's like the story that has been repeated often on the Web, but usually in a slightly skewed form. The true version is told by anthropologist Loren Eiseley, the one who wrote it, and the older man in the story. It is the story of a man walking along the shore. As he looked down the beach he saw someone moving like a dancer. He smiled to himself at the thought of someone who would dance to the day, and so, he walked faster to catch up. As he got closer, he noticed that the figure was that of a young man, and that he was not dancing at all. The young man was reaching down to the sand, picking up small objects, and throwing them into the ocean.

As he approached the young man he called out, "Good morning! May I ask what it is that you are doing?" The young man paused, looked up, and replied, "Throwing starfish into the ocean."

"I must ask, then, why are you throwing starfish into the ocean?"

To this, the young man replied, "The sun is up and the tide is going out. If I don't throw them in, they'll die."

The older man was puzzled. "But, young man," he said, "do you not realize that there are miles and miles of beach and there are starfish all along every mile? You can't possibly make a difference!" At this, the young man bent down, picked up yet another starfish, and threw it into the ocean. As it met the water, he said, "It made a difference for that one."

Those of us who want to help save a child can go to www.IJM.org to see how we can help, individually and as a church. I hope to talk to our missions team sometime this fall to see if our church can do anything. There are a lot of "starfish" out there who need our help.

My tour with International Justice Mission included going to a transition center where a child might find how to live a new life free from abuse. We met in a secluded, gated center that also serves as a school for the rescued children. It is in the transition centers that the children can recover psychologically, physically, and spiritually, far away from pimps, brothel owners, and, in some cases, parents who sold them into slavery. The transition center has a full-time physician as well as counselors on staff. All of the staff members love the children deeply.

Some of these children were arrested for petty thievery. IJM saved them from going into prison, fearing that the prisons would not only be unsafe for them but might train them to be lifelong criminals. Some were sexually abused by relatives and sometimes even by the police. Some were beaten horribly at home. IJM and other agencies saved them and the transition centers become a safe haven for them.

Some of the kids will never see their parents again because it was their parents who sold them into sex slavery or illegal child labor. Recently, there was an altercation at the gate of the transition center with parents trying to steal their child back so she would not testify against her perpetrators.

Do they truly recover? Yes!

The day we visited included a special event time of arts and crafts in the outdoor courtyard. The kids were designing and painting white t-shirts—for fun and also as a way to work on a healthy self-identity. While we were there, one of the girls turned to one of my fellow visitors, drew a cross on her t-shirt, pointed to it, and said, "Truth." They get it! I attended a banquet for the young people who have graduated from an IJM program called STARS. They were abused kids. Some were forced into child prostitution and now have been rehabilitated after going through STARS. It made me think of the starfish story. These are the proverbial starfish who were rescued by the man on the beach. Even if one child is saved, it means a lot to that child. In fact, it makes a world of difference.

One of the graduates was a child that Gary Haugen hadn't seen for a very long time. The last time he saw her was when she was rescued; she was wearing heavy makeup, dressed as a prostitute in a Manila bar. Another graduate was one of the very first children in the Philippines who was saved by IJM. Her case was really difficult because it was the chief of police in her town who was molesting her. No one in the town would help her until IJM came and rescued her through the judicial system.

What does all of this mean for you and me? What can we do? Well, for starters, those among us who have a heart for children who are at risk or trapped in poverty can keep on supporting them and writing them through Compassion International. Praise God that our church supports more than five hundred children through Compassion International as well as two other child-survival projects.

For others of us, the ministry is right at home. Some of us have children who are difficult to parent. They may be fighting an addiction to pornography, alcohol, or drugs. Sometimes they run away, either literally or figuratively. And so we must keep the symbolic porch light on, praying and hoping that someday they will come back. No matter how difficult it may be, we must keep the candle burning in the window as we look for the prodigal son or daughter to come home. Hear the word of God today: Do not grow weary in doing good. Do *not* grow weary!

Many of you can remind yourselves that what you do in your job is your ministry. The workplace is your mission field. Is there something you can do or are doing that you need to keep on doing because it is for the sake of God and you may be the only person who will tell and show fellow workers that God loves them? Do not grow weary in doing good.

Our marriages are arenas for loving and serving as well. Are we doing all that we can for our spouses? Do not grow weary in doing good. And here at church there are many ministry positions waiting to be filled by our members. Part of the church's job is to make sure you know where you can plug in. Part of your responsibility is to seek a place to participate. On the last Sunday of the month we are having a ministry fair in the fellowship hall. We will have displays and sign-ups for all of the ministry spots where you can be active and do good, including areas where we desperately need help. Should you not find a spot there, we will try to create a place that is good for you and the church. Do not grow weary in doing good.

Finally I ask, "When can we see the fruits of not growing weary?" The last part of our verse today tells the answer: "Let us not become weary in doing good, for at the proper time *we will reap a harvest if we do not give up.*" Or to put it another way, if we do not *quit* or *give up* in doing good, we will show forth God's kingdom in this world, a bountiful harvest of good.

When I joined the tour with Gary Haugen, Gary had just come back from Cambodia. He was aglow with what had just happened there. Four years ago, when he was last in Cambodia, he was on a street in Svay Pak near Phnom Penh that was full of brothels. It was a dangerous place, and he and others were there to rescue girls from prostitution. It was IJM's most successful operation to date—thirty-seven girls were rescued. But they discovered that at least a dozen or more victims had been spirited away and hidden by the brothel keepers before they got there. It was heartbreaking to know that a dozen young girls were still out there being violated.

One girl (I'll call her Mary) had been moved by the brothel owner that very day to another area. Mary, a child prostitute like Rahab in the Old Testament story of Jericho, had secretly helped in the surveillance of the place to free her friends. IJM had promised they would come to free Mary and her friends, but when they arrived she was gone. Gary's heart ached for all these years. They saved thirty-seven girls, but Mary was not among them.

But Gary did not grow weary in doing good. Through IJM he continued to engage in operations to rescue and minister to children. And two months ago—on the day before I met with him—Gary went to that same street in Svay Pak and was astonished to see that the area had been completely cleaned up. It was now perfectly safe. He couldn't believe it, but the operations that IJM had done together with law enforcement agencies led to the closing of all the brothels. When he went to the location of the brothel where they saved the thirty-seven children, he found that it was now called "Rahab's Place." No longer a brothel, it was now a halfway house run by Christians, a place of recovery for women and girls who had been in prostitution.

Then he saw her. Mary! Mary was there, now helping other girls. She had been rescued by IJM on a different raid in a different city in the brothel she was moved to. It had come full circle. Mary recovered from her ordeal and was now helping others recover from the trauma she went through and was leading them to Christ.

Friends, what can I say again but this: Do not become weary in doing good, for the harvest—like a Mary—is rich and ready . . . if only we don't give up. Whatever challenge you are facing today, God is telling you not to grow weary in doing good. Do not give up.

Amen? Amen!

24

Exhibiting the Kingdom . . . to the World

Fairfax F. Fair

*"When the Son of man comes in his glory, and all the angels with
him, then he will sit on the throne of his glory. All the nations will be
gathered before him, and he will separate people one from another
as a shepherd separates the sheep from the goats, and he will put the
sheep at his right hand and the goats at the left. Then the king will say
to those at his right hand, 'Come, you that are blessed by my Father,
inherit the kingdom prepared for you from the foundation of the world;
for I was hungry and you gave me food, I was thirsty and you gave
me something to drink, I was a stranger and you welcomed me, I was
naked and you gave me clothing, I was sick and you took care of me,
I was in prison and you visited me.' Then the righteous will answer
him, 'Lord, when was it that we saw you hungry and gave you food, or
thirsty and gave you something to drink? And when was it that we saw
you a stranger and welcomed you, or naked and gave you clothing?
And when was it that we saw you sick or in prison and visited you?'
And the king will answer them, 'Truly I tell you, just as you did it to
the least of these who are members of my family, you did it to me.'"*
Matt. 25:31–40

Let the same mind be in you that was in Christ Jesus,
*   who, though he was in the form of God,*
*   did not regard equality with God*
*   as something to be exploited,*
*   but emptied himself,*
*   taking the form of a slave,*
*   being born in human likeness.*
*   And being found in human form,*
*   he humbled himself*
*   and became obedient to the point of death—*
*   even death on a cross.*

Therefore God also highly exalted him
  and gave him the name
  that is above every name,
so that at the name of Jesus
  every knee should bend,
  in heaven and on earth and under the earth,
and every tongue should confess
  that Jesus Christ is Lord
  to the glory of God the Father.

Phil. 2:5–11

*W*hen the doorbell rang, shortly after 9:00 a.m., I was surprised to open the front door and see an older woman whom I hardly knew, wearing a big, floppy hat and holding a child's sand bucket and plastic shovel. "I've come to play with Walker," she announced, meaning my two-year-old son whose father had died upstairs in our house just a few hours earlier. For the rest of the morning, the woman and my son sat in the backyard, digging in the dirt, planting tiny seeds, and watching the clouds float by. Her name was Jo, and she was the church that morning, exhibiting the kingdom of Heaven to a fatherless little boy.

Today, another little boy lies in a big-city hospital in drug-induced paralysis while the church in places all around the country prays for the success of tedious surgery and upholds his parents as they live through an ordeal that began at his birth three years ago.

In the beginning of the first chapter of the *Book of Order*, part 2 of the Presbyterian Church's constitution, there is a short paragraph headed "The Great Ends of the Church." There, in language typical of 1910 when they were adopted, are the chief purposes of the church. Have you ever wondered why Presbyterians think God needs a church? Ever questioned why Jesus says to Simon Peter, "On this rock I will build my church"? Ever pondered why God's Spirit constitutes us into a people, called by God, to be the body of Christ? Ever considered what our mission is?

Earlier this month a team from our congregation—our ninth—made the seven-hundred-mile trip to New Orleans to continue to help its hard-hit citizens recover from the devastation of Hurricane Katrina. During this past week our building was used by over eight hundred nonmembers as they came for support groups, English classes, and other caring ministries. Downstairs in our dining room during the church-school hour this morning, a group of people presented a report on their recent trip to a small village in Nicaragua. There they worked and worshiped alongside strangers who became partners and friends.

What is all of this about?

The "Great Ends of the Church"—there are six of them—are "the proclamation of the gospel for the salvation of humankind; the shelter, nurture, and spiritual fellowship of the children of God; the maintenance of divine worship; the preservation of the truth; the promotion of social righteousness; and the exhibition of the Kingdom of Heaven to the world." Joe Small notes that, "Each of the first five is a way of exhibiting the Kingdom . . . to the world." The six together are something of a checklist for the church collectively and for each of us individually:

How are we doing at having the mind of Christ among ourselves, seeking not our personal gain or aggrandizement but a humble spirit, the desire to serve, the willingness to be servant to one another? How will we fare when we are called to account for our lives—how we have spent our time, what we have devoted our energies to, by what means we have proclaimed the gospel, cared for our fellow children of God, devoted ourselves to the worship of God, remained true to the truth of Jesus Christ, and lived the kind of social righteousness we are charged with promoting? And how are we doing with exhibiting the kingdom of Heaven to the world? Do we give it any thought? Does thinking in this way about our responsibility as Christians give us pause?

Elsewhere in the *Book of Order* we learn that the church "is the provisional demonstration of what God intends for all of humanity." Lest we think we can hide behind brick and mortar, we who are the church are the people of God—you, and I, and all of us together. Perhaps being the church is a more weighty matter than we sometimes recognize.

In the Gospel of Matthew, Jesus concludes his ministry by drawing a dramatic picture of all the peoples of the world gathering before him. Methodically, people are sorted: the righteous from the unrighteous; those who exhibited the kingdom in their daily lives and those who did not. Cries of surprise rise from both groups. From one side comes the question "We showed compassion for Jesus? How?" From the other side comes "We spurned Jesus? When?"

Two weeks ago, our sanctuary was packed. The glorious good news we celebrated as Easter people is still true, despite our diminished crowd this morning. The call to live as Easter people is still incumbent upon us. We are to live in the love of God, a love that transforms us and changes the way we treat those around us—*all* those around us.

Same Kind of Different as Me is a book about the unlikely friendship between two men—a homeless ex-con and an art dealer—and the woman who loved them both. Deborah was a wealthy woman who, in her fifties, decides to volunteer at Fort Worth's Union Gospel Mission. Her husband (the art dealer) begrudgingly goes along. As they drive through a dark tunnel and pull into the parking lot for the first time, Deborah tells her husband, "I picture this place differently than it is now. . . . No vagrants, no trash in the gutters, just a beautiful place where these people can know God loves them as much as . . . the people on the other side of that tunnel." Over time, the place was transformed—as were the lives of Deborah, her husband, and those they served. The couple gave of themselves not to gain God's favor but out of the joy of giving.

Several weeks ago—as I was just beginning to think about this sermon on the exhibition of the kingdom of Heaven to all the world—I was informed of an unexpected gift that the church had just received. It came with seemingly simple instructions that disguised a very demanding task: "Use this where it will do the most good."

> In a world of need in a sunken economy;
> In a growing church housed in an aging building;
>> in a congregation with seniors who need attention,
>> and children who need education,
>> and youth who need direction,
>> and adults who need encouragement,
>> and mission partners whose budgets have been cut;
> in a community where demand is outpacing supply for food assistance,
>> where unemployment keeps rising,
>> and people are forced to decide between medicines and electricity;
> *where can this gift do the most good*?

Where can Highland Presbyterian Church best use these dollars to exhibit the kingdom of Heaven to all the world? What if each of us were to personalize this question and then weigh our response? What if all of us were to commit a certain sum—of time or money—to making God's grace manifest to those around us? Where would we begin? *Would* we begin?

Jesus says, "I was hungry and you gave me food, I was thirsty and you gave me something to drink, I was a stranger and you welcomed me." Who here could not give another a sandwich, a cup of water, a friendly hello? Jesus is not demanding that we move mountains, or repay the staggering national debt, or find a cure for cancer. Jesus is talking about simple kindnesses that are within the capability of all of us. We can speak respectfully to everyone we meet and even greet them with a smile. We can stop to listen to a child or an older adult. We can make a phone call to someone we miss seeing in worship. We can write a note to one of the youth who led us in worship last week or to a child who sang with the children's music ministry last Wednesday evening.

Jesus is asked, "When, Lord, did we see you hungry or thirsty or a stranger?" In Jesus' day, as now, many of us live in a world filled with invisible people. Do we see the people who clerk in the pharmacy, stock the shelves of our grocery store, pass us on the sidewalk? If we do not see them, we cannot know what weighs heavy on their hearts—the strain in a marriage, the rebellion of a teen, the illness of a loved one, the loss of a job. If we do not see them, are we missing the face of Christ? Are we missing our calling to show them the love of Christ?

There are three ways to give: out of duty, to get credit, or out of love. Giving out of duty is mechanistic. It is done not for joy but to satisfy an explicit or implicit requirement. Giving to get credit is giving to get something back. It is selfishness masquerading as generosity. Giving out of love is the only giving that is genuine and heart-felt and that exhibits the kingdom of Heaven. It is this kind of love that is the great end of the church and the heart of the gospel.

Friends, we are called to exhibit the kingdom of Heaven to all the world: without checking identification or cleanliness; without checking for literacy or lice; without verification of address or pedigree. The only qualification for our help is need. We exhibit the kingdom by showing the love of God because it has been shown to us: through ladies with plastic sand buckets, teams with hammers, people with hearts of love. Together, let us exhibit God's kingdom, here and now, to all the world.

To God be all glory, honor, and praise, world without end. Amen.

ACKNOWLEDGMENTS

Joseph D. Small, *The Great Ends of the Church: Short-Term Study Course for Adults* (Louisville, KY: Witherspoon Press, 2006).

Ron Hall and Denver Moore with Lynn Vincent, *Same Kind of Different as Me* (Nashville: Thomas Nelson, 2006).

Contributors

Jerry Andrews is pastor of First Presbyterian Church, San Diego, California. He previously served congregations in Glen Ellyn, Illinois, and Hookstown, Pennsylvania.

Tom Are Jr. is pastor of Village Presbyterian Church, Prairie Village, Kansas.

Heidi Husted Armstrong is interim pastor of Trinity Presbyterian Church, Tacoma, Washington. She previously served as Christian Impact Director at World Vision U.S.A.

M. Craig Barnes is pastor of Shadyside Presbyterian Church, Pittsburgh, Pennsylvania, and Robert Meneilly Professor of Leadership and Ministry, Pittsburgh Theological Seminary.

Peter B. Barnes is pastor of Westlake Hills Presbyterian Church, Austin, Texas. He previously served congregations in Boulder, Colorado; Dallas, Texas; and Alexandria, Virginia.

Deborah Block is pastor of Immanuel Presbyterian Church, Milwaukee, Wisconsin.

Jerry Cannon is pastor of C. N. Jenkins Presbyterian Church, Charlotte, North Carolina.

Christine Chakoian is pastor of First Presbyterian Church, Lake Forest, Illinois.

Dan Chun is pastor of First Honolulu Presbyterian Church, Kaneohe, Hawaii.

Chris Currie is pastor of Calypso Presbyterian Church, Calypso, North Carolina.

Fairfax F. Fair is pastor of Highland Presbyterian Church, Louisville, Kentucky.

Veronica R. Goines is pastor of Saint Andrew Presbyterian Church, Marin City, California.

Timothy D. Hart-Andersen is pastor of Westminster Presbyterian Church, Minneapolis, Minnesota.

Jennifer Oraker Holz is associate pastor of First Presbyterian Church, Colorado Springs, Colorado.

Jin S. Kim is pastor of the Church of All Nations, Columbia Heights, Minnesota.

Mark Labberton is Lloyd John Ogilvie Associate Professor of Preaching, Fuller Theological Seminary. He previously served as pastor of First Presbyterian Church, Berkeley, California.

Michael L. Lindvall is pastor of the Brick Presbyterian Church, New York, New York.

Rodger Nishioka is Benton Family Associate Professor of Christian Education, Columbia Theological Seminary.

K. C. Ptomey Jr. is Louis S. & Katherine H. Zbinden Professor of Pastoral Ministry and Leadership, Austin Presbyterian Theological Seminary. He previously served as pastor of Westminster Presbyterian Church, Nashville, Tennessee.

Elizabeth McGregor Simmons is pastor of Davidson College Presbyterian Church, Davidson, North Carolina.

Joseph D. Small is Director of Theology Worship and Education Ministries, Presbyterian Church (U.S.A.). He previously served congregations in Rochester, New York; Westerville, Ohio; and Towson, Maryland.

Theodore J. Wardlaw is president and Professor of Homiletics, Austin Presbyterian Theological Seminary. He previously served as pastor of Central Presbyterian Church, Atlanta, Georgia.

Scott Weimer is pastor of North Avenue Presbyterian Church, Atlanta, Georgia.

K. Nicholas Yoda is pastor of Pleasant Ridge Presbyterian Church, Cincinnati, Ohio.